ECOLOGY OF WAR & PEACE

Counting Costs of Conflict

Tom H. Hastings

University Press of America
Lanham • New York • Oxford

4720 Boston Way
Lanham, Maryland 20706

12 Hid's Copse Rd.
Cumnor Hill, Oxford OX2 9JJ

Printed in the United States of America
British Library Cataloging in Publication Information Available

ISBN 0-7618-1787-5 (cloth: alk. ppr.)
ISBN 0-7618-1788-3 (pbk: alk. ppr.)

™ The paper used in this publication meets the minimum requirements of American National Standard for Information Sciences—Permanence of Paper for Printed Library Materials, ANSI Z39.48—1984

For the memory of Whitefeather of the Ojibwe and for every other nonviolent warrior who has paid a sacrificial price in defense of Creation.

contents~~~

preface~~~

I was a high school kid when the Tet Offensive hit and I graduated in June of 1968, as the body bags were returning—older brothers, cousins, the track star from three years ago—if you were an American kid, you knew someone who was in pain from that war.

Then I moved into the working world and took my chances filing for a conscientious objector status, which I eventually got. As a manual laborer, I had plenty of buddies with shrapnel in them, drugs in them, fear in them, hatred in them. They told me of river trips and shooting everything in a 360-degree arc at every twig snap or leaf rustle. I began to understand just how much terror war can send sweeping through hearts and minds of warriors and civilians alike; it is a whirlwind of horror. Concern for the Earth is essentially irrelevant to a person suffering from suffocating fear for personal survival or survival of loved ones.

Vietnam War combat vet and author Tim O'Brien, in a 1990 interview with radio host Terry Gross, told of watching some fellow troops turn on a baby water buffalo and fire untold numbers of bullets into that innocent, harmless creature, all from a strangling sense of raw, goading fear of becoming "meat." The rage was expended on that baby and that baby is the Earth, and that baby is your baby, and that baby is why I have been in the peace movement for more than three decades, and that baby is why I wrote this book. I fervently hope that it edges us some tiny step closer to the day when that baby is no longer a target, but rather is regarded universally as protected. That baby is the true, hidden cost of war that we have ignored too long, that we are beginning to appreciate, and that we need to count against the notion of waging or preparing to wage war.

Literally, no one can take your place in this battle to assess war and then to learn more practical ways to manage conflict. You are the one. I am the one. We are the ones. That baby is hoping. Let's not let her down.

—Tom H. Hastings, Maple, Wisconsin, April 2000

acknowledgments~~~

Without Dr. Kent Shifferd, I would never have pursued this field with even a remotely academic approach. He is a mentor and he's helped me with my many errors, though I persist in some, without doubt. In addition, Dr. Andy Goyke, Dr. Thomas J. Hastings, Susan Hall, Grant Herman, Paula Hyde, Jill Lance, John Maxwell, Pat Miller, Hilary Pollack, Mary Rehwald, Craig Shanks, Laura Watt and Dr. Chris Wells have read and graciously commented on all or on sections, helping me immeasurably. The omissions and errors remaining are mine.

Caring about, learning about and acting in defense of the Earth is fostered and supported by the institution where I have the privilege to teach, Northland, an environmental liberal arts college. The students, staff, faculty, trustees and administration are committed to the environmental mission of the school and to the program I coördinate, Peace, Conflict and Global Studies.

The nonviolent resisters—from Phil Berrigan and Donna Howard, on back to Mohandas K. Gandhi, Dorothy Day and Dr. Martin Luther King Jr.—many of whom are serving prison sentences in rogue nations such as Cuba, Libya, Syria, *Greece, Turkey, Australia and the United States,* all challenge me to put a human face on suffering, to take that suffering seriously, to suggest that a warrior need not be violent, and then to strive harder to put care for the Earth in more hearts.

My father, Dr. Thomas J. Hastings, taught me that we must be good campers; we keep the campsite clean for the Next Ones. This lesson, from trips through mountains and by the shores of Gitchii Guumii for almost half a century, formulated my values about the Earth. "Doc Sarvis" Hastings has been my enduring supporter from the day I decided to become a conscientious objector to war. We've proceeded on loving, parallel paths ever since.—T.H.H.

acronyms~~~

AEC: Atomic Energy Commission
AFSC: American Friends Service Committee
AIDS: acquired immune deficiency syndrome
AIM: American Indian Movement
A/NZ: Aotearoa/New Zealand
ANZUS: Australia New Zealand United States (military alliance)
B.C.E.: before the common era
BTF: Balkans Task Force
BTX: botulinum toxin
CDB: civilian-based defense
CIA: Central Intelligence Agency
CTBT: Comprehensive Test Ban Treaty
CSWAB: Citizens for Safe Water Around Badger
CW: Catholic Worker
DoD: Department of Defense
DOE: Department of Energy
DU: depleted uranium
EDSA:
ELF: extremely low frequency (radio signal)
EMP: electromagnetic pulse
EMR: electromagnetic radiation
ESA: Endangered Species Act
FBI: Federal Bureau of Investigation
FOR: Fellowship of Reconciliation
FRY: Federal Republic of Yugoslavia
FSU: former Soviet Union
GATT: General Agreement on Trade and Tariffs
GNP: gross national product
INGO: international non-governmental organization
HAARP: high-frequency active auroral research program
ICJ: International Court of Justice
IDF: Israeli Defense Force
MIA: missing in action
MT: megaton
MWFEP: Ministry of Waters, Forests and Environmental Protection

(Romania)
NAFTA: North American Free Trade Association
NASA: National Aeronautics and Space Administration
NATO: North Atlantic Treaty Organization
NGO: non-governmental organization
NIMBY: not in my backyard
NOPE: not on planet Earth
NRC: Nuclear Regulatory Commission
NYC: New York city
OSCE: Organization for Security and Cooperation in Europe
PCBs: polychlorinated biphenyls
PSR: Physicians for Social Responsibility
PTBT: Partial Test Ban Treaty
SCUD:
SIPI: Scientists Institute for Public Information
START: strategic arms reductions treaty
STD: sexually transmitted disease
STRATCOM: Strategic Command
SU: Soviet Union
UK: United Kingdom
ULIMO-J and ULIMO-K:
UN: United Nations
UNCHS: UN Centre for Human Settlements
UNEP: United Nations Environmental Programme
UNHCR: United Nations High Commissioner for Refugees
US: United States
USAF: United States Air Force
USSR: United Soviet Socialist Republics (Soviet Union)
WAND: Women's Action for Nuclear Disarmament
WHO: World Health Organization
WRL: War Resisters League
WTF: Wisconsin Test Facility
WTO: World Trade Organization

Introduction: Spoils of war

Politicians are the ultimate creatures of the moment. Their post confronts them with a constant stream of problems that must be solved now, without regard for next year....

Better to wage a quick, clean "war" on something....That requires much less perspicacity than trying to solve long-term social problems and is much more likely to lead to reëlection....The perceptual horizon of politicians tends to be confined in space as well as in time....Officials still weigh the effects of their actions on national security in a world in which global security is at risk.

—Robert Ornstein & Paul Ehrlich (Ornstein: 151)

A thing is right when it tends to preserve the integrity, stability, and beauty of the biotic community. It is wrong when it tends otherwise.

—Aldo Leopold (Leopold: 262)

By Leopold's definition, it ought to be easy to show that war is wrong; since the time of the Ancients we have known that the integrity, stability and beauty of the biota, Life, is damaged and destroyed by war. (Westing: 24) We are now learning that, by Leopold's dictum, humanity ought to forswear the preparation for war. *Si pacem, para bellum*—"If you want peace, prepare for war"—may have served some rulers quite admirably down through the ages. But that preparation is killing vast sectors of the biosphere, that layer of the Earth from the benthos to the mountaintops, the slender slice of the planet that actually contains living organisms.

War is misanthropic. War is anthropogenic. War is thus an oxymoronic activity. This book argues that war and the preparation for war are so maladaptive nowadays that we simply don't deserve our self-anointed title, *Homo sapiens*—the wise ones. A wise species survives. A wise species doesn't annihilate itself and ruin its living quarters, which is what war and war readiness are doing. A wise species adapts rather than obdurately and pertinaciously clinging to an outmoded strategy that is itself a greater threat than its promised protection from threat. We have a new need: *Si pacem, para pacem.*

We are like flies, says Gordy Fellman, crawling around on the ceiling of the Sistine Chapel, with little vision or understanding of the angels or gods who lay beneath and above our threshold of perception. (Fellman: 227) We try to gain perspective but we struggle with the breadth of it. This little book cannot be comprehensive; the problems of war and the depth of hope of its elimination are far too massive a body of interrelated information. One of our premier analysts in the Peace Studies interdiscipline, Thomas F. Homer-Dixon of the Peace and Conflict Studies program, University of Toronto, simply noted, "Unfortunately, the environment-security theme encompasses an almost unmanageable array of sub-issues, especially if we define 'security' broadly to include human physical, social, and economic well-being." (Homer-Dixon, part 1: 1) This book merely touches upon representative elements of this region of study and the hope is that it makes a contribution to the literature, a bit of an advance in understanding.

Every book, every text, proceeds from assumptions. The bias in this study is toward nonviolence and an abolition of war. I make no pretext, then, of objectivity and my language advocates toward nonviolence, toward the abolition of war and war preparation. For this I make no apology; I am convinced that this is the point from which the field of Peace Studies ought to *begin*. The question is never, "Where is violence appropriate?" but rather, "How do we mitigate and eventually eliminate all violence?" I *do* apologize in advance to the reader for whom my efforts at persuasion cross the line to hortatory; my many years as an editorial columnist are in constant tension with both my journalist and academic training. I spent some years in the practice of journalism and have a graduate degree in that field. I am also an activist and my journalism inevitably tends toward advocacy. As some comfort to those readers, I'm also trained to sniff out factual hyperbole and I believe this work is as free of it as I can make it.

While we are rightly suspect of slippery slope arguments, human psychology suggests that the old style of diplomacy will lead to violence, sooner or later. That is, when violence is threatened, it ultimately, at some point, needs to be committed. If not, credibility suffers. That is a part of the double bind of nuclear weapons; when we threaten the unthinkable, the opponent can tell us, "you aren't really thinking that. After all, you call it unthinkable." Simply, the demands of rational statecraft impel belligerents to prove their irrationality periodically. Is this a sustainable, wise system of conflict management?

This means, at the very least, that nations which accept violence as a legitimate method of conflict management—virtually all nations—must then prepare for war. The best of them only prepare defensively. The worst call it defense but build offensive weaponry on the theory used by hockey coaches and chess players alike, "the best defense is a good offense." We can call it the Department of Defense, but when it is forward-based around the world and comprises the only nuclear arsenal in this parsec of deep space capable of a decapitating first-strike against any conceivable opponent, we have to confess to its offensive nature. It is ironic that, at the beginning of the Cold War, as the US military in particular entered both the forward-basing and nuclear modes—that is, offensively oriented toward the rest of the world—its name changed from the War Department to the Department of Defense. That began a seriously spun-unto-twisted posture.

Only since the end of the Cold War have we begun to tentatively assess the attack made on the Earth from behind the cloak of "national security." There has been some *glasnost*, some openness, in the US and former Soviet Union. We know that Lake Karachay in the FSU is so radioactive from it military nuclear waste that it is evaporated and, if some family on a picnic sat by its former banks for an hour, they would absorb a lifetime dose of radiation. We know that the US Army tested animals and humans to see what radiation would do, in order to assess how much fighting a soldier could accomplish after exposure and before incapacitation and death. We know that the DoD is responsible for more than 50 Superfund sites and more than 14,000 environmental "hotspots." (Thomas: 9) The accretion of such information is gradually assembling into a picture of the military as a significant threat to "the standard of living to which we've become accustomed," i.e., breathable air and drinkable water. To begin the process of addressing this 45-year abuse on a massive scale, congress finally passed the Federal Facility Compliance Act in late 1992; while this didn't cover the tremendous damage done off-base by the military, nor did it assign any responsibility toward the companies that profited while they polluted, it was a beginning.

It is easy for a ruler whose subjects are innumerable and whose authority is iron-fisted-absolute to get away with such threats—his own people don't count politically or physically. But a great democracy must veil those threats, and we do. Then, periodically, the velvet gloves come off and the iron fist of the state's arsenal comes down hard.

The negotiators carry big sticks and their diplomacy is lethal. When the war in Bosnia drew in American helpers, the first thing they did was to call air strikes. At the express behest of "negotiators" Strobe Talbot and Richard Holbrooke, the missiles flew. On 30 August 1995, "Operation Deliberate Force" pummeled Bosnian Serb positions around Sarajevo, the largest NATO military action in history. (Holbrooke: 101) Turns out to have been a warm-up act. At some point the most heavily armed nation-state in human history finds it imperative to unleash a devastating attack, just to remind itself and the world that it still can. In a way, the 1999 bombing of Belgrade was a natural extension of the Dayton Accords of 1995, and that is not atypical. The so-called "peace accords" arrived at by belligerents Slobodan Milošević and Alija Izetbegović under the wing of the US not only forced a solution glaringly biased toward Serb expansionist aims, but also cut out the only nonviolent political force in the region, Ibrahim Rugova's Kosovar Albanians. In the end, the school of traditional statecraft, from von Clausewitz to Henry Kissinger to Madeleine Albright is one long story of bluff and call, armament and firepower. And in the end, we ask, who pays, who profits, who suffers, who dies, who drives away in style and whose children are born with birth defects? The answers give a hint of the true pricetag for the violent threatpower we take for granted. The perspective gained may help us recalculate the value of war and preparing for war.

In some ways, the questions about the Earth and war are about not seeing the forest for the trees. It is land, after all, over which we so often fight. Following the 1967 war in the Middle East, "the Arab world grasped that the key to regaining the territories Israel had gained in that war was to be sought in … the principle of exchanging 'land for peace.'" (Rabinovich: 7) What is so ironic is the abuse heaped upon that very land by the war machinery so intent on seizing it. That is the dilemma this book tries to illuminate and around which we hope to chart a course.

Disclaimer: this book is not only not compendious, it is not adequate. The sheer magnitude of merely *listing* all the various damages to the environment from waging and preparing to wage war is far greater than the slim volume you hold in your hands. This book does not attempt to construct that list, yet the reader determined to do so can do worse than to begin here and work through the excellent materials listed in the bibliography. It also needs to be noted that there is a natural focus on the contemporary and on the largest military in the world, that of the US. This skewed view ought not suggest that the other huge militaries are less rapacious, more caring for the Earth or any less polluting. Nothing could be further from the truth. There are mammoth environmental problems as a result of Soviet, Chinese, British, French, Canadian and other militaries. As a US citizen, teacher and activist, I am drawn to confront my own nation-state's militarism and injustice first. Which brings us to the US Department of Defense.

Where there's smoke, there are mirrors: DoD PR

> *The brass appeared, as scheduled, in full uniform, medals and all, and were asked one question. "Did the U.S. military deposit any toxic material at Love Canal?"* [Carter Chief of Staff Jack] *Watson asked. "No sir, we did not." "Thank you , gentlemen," replied Watson, and off they went....*[later, after that was proven a lie and a resident asked why] *"Because, Ma'am," replied Col. Norris, "we're in the business of protecting your country, not protecting the environment."* (Collette: 1 & 6)

> *On behalf of the American people, I commend the Department of Defense for its environmental stewardship.*—Bill Clinton, US president (Clinton)

When the Cold War ended, the endless excuse of "national security," by which the Department of Defense weaseled out of all its environmental accountability, went up in smoke. Sadly, when the clouds began to clear, the Pentagon invented a new smoke screen: "We're the environmental warriors."

It is a good thing to have the Pentagon claim transparency and eco-responsibility. That way, when they obfuscate or maneuver to avoid committing the financial resources to the problems they have generated, people who care can point to the situation, to the rhetoric, and ask about the gulf in between. This is not possible in some undemocratic places, and yet citizens of democratic nations actually have the temerity to expect others to stand up to the egregious lies of their governments while they are too apathetic or nervous to do that in a "free" system. Many in the US blamed the fearful citizens of the former Soviet Union for not confronting its huge and utterly illegal biological weapons program, but we fail to confront our own—and when the head of those Soviet programs defected to the US, did we prosecute, based on, for example, the Nuremberg precedent and the Flick case? We did not; the fellow is living openly with no sanction in Virginia, still working in biotechnology.

It is the profoundly misanthropic nature of war that we completely miss when we honor it, when we accept it, when we plan for it. From the janitor who loses a great deal of his small paycheck to the nation's military, to the scientist whose molecular biology is devoted to learning to transport genetic virulence of a bacteria via plasmids to a new microorganism, we seem to miss the basic point: we cannot prepare for war without preparing to attack the foundations of human existence. Any other interpretation of war is delusional.

The pollution of the air and water from the actions of the militaries of the world is enormous; the contamination of the decision-making process by which we decide to build huge arsenals is just as profound. It affects our very culture, the human pool in which we all swim. When the least opposition to U.S. policies is announced anywhere, the US media trumpets the most shrill and blustery voices, identifying them as the enemy. Without an enemy, any military loses its *raison d'être*, its very justification for existence. Any overview of the major media will reveal such an enemy search on an ongoing basis. Cuba is a highly vaunted foe; they devote all of one-third of one percent of the US military budget to their military (less than $1 billion compared to US $300 billion-$500 billion). Bioterrorism was featured for five days on Ted Koppel's *Nightline* (10/1/99; 10/5-8/99) but was so lacking in factual attachment to real threat that Koppel turned to fictional scenarios instead. (Kruzman: 21) Major media frequently rely on DoD consultants for advice on accuracy, but that counsel can contaminate the message, especially when DoD reserves release-blocking rights, which is common in film. Because the militaries naturally engage in worst-case-scenario analysis in order to be prepared, their fictional extrapolation is virtually identical to media hype—which jibes well with the defense industry lobbyists' efforts to justify astonishing capital outlays. Threat exaggeration is often the only rationalization for the ongoing construction and maintenance of an arsenal larger and more toxic than any ever assembled in history. We struggle to understand what our rational choices might be amidst the deluge of hyperbole.

worldwide web

This book, like any attempt at an ecology, is diversified, and its sections are interrelated, interdependent. As John Muir told us, we pick up anything in the universe and find it hitched to everything else, a worldwide web that long preceded anything electronic or cyberspacy. That's how we find all this information and observation about war, peace and the Earth, linked but not hierarchical. Still, we can look at living ecosystems in their subsystems and that is what we do in this book; there are four sections, each divided into three chapters, all ultimately more related than they are not.

The first section examines preparation for war; the environment suffers mightily from the mere production of, maintenance of, and training to use the tools of war.

The second section examines the outbreak and subsequent eco-disaster, the ecological threat of war and its machinery. Each and every war is an ecological catastrophe, historically and currently.

In the third section we look to our Earth as a threatened well that can run dry in the face of unlimited extraction. How will the resultant scarcity fuel the drive toward conflict, toward war and even toward a collapse of the current nation-state system and its ecology of war?

In the fourth section, holding the first three sections in our minds, we explore the advantages and possibilities of resolving all conflicts without violence, from the interpersonal to the international. We call this the Ecology of Peace and it is much more than an ivory tower theory; some are fighting in this way already, some have shown us techniques, tactics, strategies and philosophies. Since Biblical times humanity has tried to proscribe war damage to "vines" and orchards and the wells and springs we all need for life. (Westing: 24) We examine what others have taught, what the Earth has shown us, and how we fit in, how we can begin, in the words of Santee Sioux activist poet John Trudell, to live up to our obligations as just one species among all the rest here on Mother Earth.

Peace-oriented ecologists began to wonder about the scope of military impacts on the Earth years ago. Peace anthropologist Margaret Mead, as president of Scientists' Institute for Public Information, helped organize a study of the effects of American bombing of mangrove wetlands in Vietnam. SIPI biologists and ecologists did overflights and field research to determine at least a portion of the environmental result of the Pentagon policy of the day, called "area denial." (Pfeiffer: 37) But when the American government studied the environmental effects, those findings were buried as deeply as the toxic plumes of pollution spreading away from dumped chemicals at US bases in Vietnam. As a result of SIPI, other environmental professionals with a conscience, and an increasingly aware and aroused public, we are in a different public discourse environment nowadays. Old cynics like Slobodan Milošević have now learned to *situationally* claim environmental havoc in the hopes that public support for war against him will wane.

Ecology is defined as the relationships between organisms and their environment. Nowadays, the *political* ecology of the nation-state system—the nation-states and their global political system—is under increasing duress. "The post-cold war era," writes analyst Michael Renner, "is increasingly witnessing a phenomenon of what some have call 'failed states'—the implosion of countries like Rwanda, Somalia, Yugoslavia, and others. But they are only the spectacular victims of the pressures and vulnerabilities of the current era—underlying forces that many other countries are subjected to as well but have managed, for the time being at least, to cope with more successfully." (Renner, 1997: 117) Thus, the stability of the nation-state political ecology is evermore shaky as it is weakened by its own internal structural limitations in the face of new challenges. An existential threat to one member of the "family" of nation-states is cause for great unease amongst the rest, understandably. War is the ultimate manifestation of that existential threat to each state and thus to the entire system.

What are the anthropogenic—the human-made—causes of war? For the weakest and most unstable nation-states, we like to ascribe "ethnic hatred" as the single causal factor, intermixed with other "blame the victim" etiological claims. Isn't this phenomenon somewhat reminiscent of Big Tobacco eluding legal culpability for scores of years by managing to successfully perpetrate the Big Lie, that all the damage is the fault of the user? But those who take huge profits hold commensurate responsibility, and those who intake vast sums from governments who feel obligated or desirous of purchasing as much military might as they can are similarly accountable if we apply similar juridical standards.

To carry the analogy further, those who profit from the highly lucrative positioning that results from a heavily militarized world—those who profit from repression of labor rights in maldeveloped areas, those who profit from lax environmental law or enforcement in the same areas—are in a position of the air polluters who cast all blame on the victims: "They smoke at higher rates than the rest of the population." We are in a constant struggle to expose this chicanery and right the wrongs that it perpetuates. The notion cannot be dismissed that each human bears his or her share of the responsibility to correct the hatreds that are demonstrably a part of many conflicts; that would be the posturing of fatuous ideologues. Rather, this book suggests that we can increase our depth of field; we can move outward to a synoptic view—i.e., understanding the role of our various cultures—even as we try to sharpen our vision looking at each identifiable part of the problem, each individual. No culture should teach children to hate, pollute or kill, *and* no child should hate, pollute or kill even if taught to do so.

We learn that, for example, in 1992, Malaysia made the choice to spend much of its national treasury on two warships while the very same expenditure would have provided potable water for a quarter-century for the five million Malaysians now lacking it. (Renner, 1995: 152) This is an ecological and human health problem exacerbated by the military; the "protectors" are actually the worst thieves. Worse, the putative guardians of our land use those massive budget allocations to consume and contaminate that land's natural bounty. Historian William McNeill calls the military the original "macroparasite" and we find this a direct ecological problem, not a metaphor. The Pentagon employs more than a thousand lobbyists, all working Congress for more money, incestuously paid for by working Americans. It is a mutually reinforcing dynamic that undermines the ecological stability, the fiscal probity of the national budget, and the prudential management of the fruits of the labors of those who trust and toil, work and pay in good faith.

Another positive feedback loop of negative consequence might be called the war damage/war driver mutually reinforcing dynamic. How does the damage caused by waging war contribute to the seeds of the next conflict? War burns and churns the Earth, plowing the fertile fields for seeds of future violence, a point made cogently by historian Bernard Nietschmann. "Ultimately, ashes and mud counterinsurgency policies will be counterproductive. Degraded land and resources are as much a reason for taking up arms as are repression, invasion, and ideology." (Nietschmann: 37)

Some say that the environmental damage is literally a dirty shame, but that, since we need a robust method of national defense, we must accept that regrettable necessity. Indeed, if we are to rely on the credible threat to commit more annihilatory violence than the opponent, our list of ecological woes is merely a lugubrious litany and we are keening without a cause. Only when we in the field of Peace Studies can replace that sense of futility with a new cause for confidence in an array of better methods will our culture then care more deeply.

The shock of atomic attack on Hiroshima and Nagasaki drove the search for, and development of, conflict management theories. Now, half a century later, those developing theories are daily informed by the practice and we may at last see some hope on the horizon. When those negotiating skills are reinforced by intelligent and disciplined mass nonviolent citizen resistance to toxic militarism, we may at last be witnessing the beginning of the end of the war system. When enough people are convinced that there is hope of resolving actual conflict by means other than armed might, people are much more likely to join in a clean-up effort that will go to protecting our land *and* our freedom.

Finally, by way of introduction, I must note the severe limits of such a small book on such a big topic. The serious student will read this little volume and then start in on the many superior works listed in the bibliography. Entire military-induced environmental catastrophes go un-mentioned; this book is not comprehensive. Someone will produce the Encyclopedia of Military Ecological Effects one day, I hope. Stopping humankind's destruction of each other and of the Earth will take a lifetime of learning and application from each and every one of us.

sources

Clinton, William J., "A Message from William J. Clinton President of the United States of America," *Today: Preserving Our Environmental Future*, 1996: inside cover.

Collette, Will, ***Dealing With Military Toxics***. Falls Church VA: Citizen's Clearinghouse for Hazardous Wastes Inc., 1987.

Fellman, Gordon, ***Rambo and the Dalai Lama: The Compulsion to Win and Its Threat to Human Survival***. Albany NY: State University of New York Press, 1998.

Holbrooke, Richard, ***To End a War***. NYC: Random House, Modern Library, 1999.

Homer-Dixon, Thomas F., "On the Threshold: Environmental Changes as Causes of Acute Conflict," *International Security* 16:2 (Fall 1991) (76-116) reprinted on Thomas F. Homer-Dixon website in three parts plus endnotes.

Kruzman, Roni, "Koppel's "Biowar of the Worlds," in *Extra!*, January-February 2000: 21.

Leopold, Aldo, ***A Sand Country Almanac***. NYC: Ballantine Books, 1966 (original Oxford University Press, 1949).

Nietschmann, Bernard, "Battlefields of Ashes and Mud," in *Natural History*, November 1990: 35-37.

Ornstein, Robert, and Paul Ehrlich, ***New World New Mind: Moving Toward Conscious Evolution*** NYC: Doubleday, 1989.

Pfeiffer, E.W., "Degreening Vietnam," in *Natural History*, November 1990: 37-40.

Rabinovich, Itamar, ***Waging Peace: Israel and the Arabs and the End of the Century***. NYC: Farrar, Strauss and Giroux, 1999.

Renner, Michael, "Budgeting for Disarmament," in: Worldwatch Institute, ***State of the World 1995***. New York: W.W. Norton & Company Ltd., 1995: 150-169.

Renner, Michael, "Transforming Security," in: Worldwatch Institute, ***State of the World 1997***. New York: W.W. Norton & Company Ltd., 1997: 115-131.

Thomas, William, ***Scorched Earth: The Military's Assault on the Environment***. Gabriola Island, Vancouver, British Columbia: New Society Press, 1995.

Section 1: Ecological Costs of War Readiness

> *Each day the hope that our countries will receive as much aid for human development as they once received for militarization grows increasingly remote.*
>
> —Oscar Arias, former President of Costa Rica, 1987 Nobel Peace Laureate (Renner, 1995: 158)

The total sum of effects of war and war preparation upon the environment will never be known. It is a massive and daily accumulating disaster. From the ancient Romans who ordered the salting of fields in Carthage in order to exact punitive sanctions at the conclusion of the Punic Wars more than 2,100 years ago, to the medieval war practice of dumping diseased human and animal carcasses into wells, and from the deforestation of the Mediterranean in no small part to build ships of war in ancient days, or to the taking of the virgin stands of ancient white pine in New England to make British warships in the eighteenth century, warmaking has taken the best and polluted the rest. This examination is a short one and the list is long. The object is to begin to challenge ourselves to examine the worthiness of the war paradigm with the Earth in mind as another inevitable casualty.

The common etymological origin of our "ecology" and "economy," from the Greek *oiko*, meaning "home," or "house," ought to guide us back to the ineluctable connections we "civilized" peoples strive to forget; our economy (monetary relationships) is, in the end, utterly dependent upon the ecology (living organisms' relationship to each other and the Earth). We cannot get either house in order without understanding the roles and results of military scope and activity.

Taking a historical view with the questions about the ecological effects of the military shines new light on old situation and may raise legitimate questions, from macro to the micro. Was the European holocaust of the

13th-15th centuries—the various plagues that decimated entire populations—spread by war? Has typhus been a major human ecological problem mostly due to war? Has the tragic history of sexually transmitted disease been largely due to the activities of troops—mobile, rapacious and generally sexually active from population to population—and pushing refugees across nations to contract and then inflict STDs themselves—throughout history? What new questions do we need to ask of history in order to explore this field more accurately, more tellingly, in order to assess the true costs of this model of conflict management in the human experiment?

The ambition of the militaries, serviced by the science of the day, literally knows no bounds. In the 12th century the military science of the day sought to raze the stone walls of city-states or somehow kill all those within. They developed both cannon and biological warfare. By the modern era, given quantum leaps in available technology, there was actually a serious proposal made by Edward Teller's boys at Lawrence Livermore Laboratory to "excavate" a harbor at Cape Thompson, Alaska, using six thermonuclear bombs—Teller's "Project Chariot." (Begich: 114) The brakes on the abuse of the Earth and all Her creatures have historically been applied by an informed and active citizenry, if at all.

sources

Begich, Dr. Nick and Jeane Manning, ***Angels Don't Play This HAARP: Advances in Tesla Technology***. Anchorage AK: 1995.

Renner, Michael, "Budgeting for Disarmament," in: Worldwatch Institute, ***State of the World 1995***. New York: W.W. Norton & Company Ltd., 1995: 150-169.

Renner, Michael, "Transforming Security," in: Worldwatch Institute, ***State of the World 1997***. New York: W.W. Norton & Company Ltd., 1997: 115-131.

Pax Atomica: poisonous preparation

It is one of the great ironies of our age: in the name of protecting our national security and well-being, we are poisoning ourselves. Every day, government facilities involved in producing nuclear weapons spew toxic pollutants into our environment. (Coyle: 11)

In my work as a social worker … I entered the family's home, I told the man that he would not get any groceries this time because of the income…. He was a huge man who had worked in a tannery…. He locked the door, drew down the blind, took up a butcher knife.... He said that he would carve me up … that he had locked up … other relief workers … even if he had to do time in the workhouse … after an hour … I reached out my hand … saying, "You are all right…. I am not afraid of that false face you have on. I see the good man inside. If you want to knife me or knock me cold, go ahead. I won't hit you back; go ahead, I dare you!"

But I didn't double dare him.

– Ammon Hennacy (Hennacy: 48)

Deterrence and confrontation are dicey businesses; what has waving atomic knives and bellowing dire annihilatory threats done to humankind and our Earth? We have dared the demons. When will our acquiescence, our passivity, become a double dare? Even after the *Washington Post* blew the whistle on the Pentagon's nuclear weapon's uranium plant in Paducah, Kentucky, even after that news of "radioactive-waste dumps, safety violations, bureaucratic lies, cancer, environmental pollution" and plutonium exposure for decades, the citizenry were mostly avoiding the issue. (Mason: 31) They seemed to feel, some said, as though the mere acknowledgment of the lethal harm that had already taken lives in their midst might cause the shutdown of their "bomb plant." (Mason: 31) Daniel Ellsberg, upon reviewing the data taken in every US poll published on nuclear weapons questions between 1945-1984, concluded that

"Americans would rather drive to the Holocaust in a Cadillac." (Ellsberg)

In keeping with Ellsberg's finding, *The New Yorker* writer Bobbie Ann Mason calls the silence of the injured Paducah locals a "social contract," in which the job gives high pay and a steady check and the band of employees gives permission to pollute, "the social contract meant getting along by going along. The problem was that the plant had been a good neighbor. It was good to its workers, who kept the secret well." (Mason: 36) Thus, even though the citizens of Paducah—most of whom had either worked at the bomb plant or whose family members had—knew that they were exposed to plutonium radiation counts as high as 500 picocuries (33 times what the Pentagon had called acceptable in open-air tests in the South Pacific), they accepted it as their part of the *quid pro quo*. (Mason: 34) It seems as though workers' sense of self-worth has been sufficiently linked to the lie of noble sacrifice and the other lie that workplace conditions are what we accept along with the job, so that those ties do bind their hands from involvement in stopping this eco-tragedy, this assault on the health of working people and their families. Without a change in this attitude, then, the children of Paducah and the generations of humans and wildlife in that area are simply "acceptable losses." To the extent that this exists across the US and the world, a block to a change exists. To the extent that people understand that loyalty ought not extend to employers and governments who poison them, their children and the Earth, we can force a way through those blocks.

> *The capacity for human error, human failure, mechanical failure, misunderstanding, was virtually infinite. I have seen nuclear airplanes crash under circumstances that were designed to replicate, but were inevitably far less stressful than, the actual condition of nuclear war. I have seen human error lead to the explosion of missiles in the silos. I have read the circumstances of submarines going to the bottom of the ocean laden with nuclear missiles and warheads because of failures, mechanical flaws, and human error. I read that entire history, and when I came away from it – because I was never given access to it before – I was chilled. I was chilled to the depths of my strategic soul.*
> – General George Lee Butler (USAF, Ret.)

General George Lee Butler writes of what he learned as he rose through the ranks of strategic nuclear command, all the way to the very top, until he was military commander of all of America's strategic nuclear forces—all the intercontinental nuclear weapons with which this nation is supposed to wage international nuclear war. His command was over STRATCOM—Strategic Command—based in Omaha, Nebraska. That post gave him command over the missiles in the underground silos, the bombs on board strategic aircraft and over the sea leg of the triad. That ocean-going arsenal contains the bulk of US America's strategic nuclear forces, those on Trident, Poseidon and Polaris "boomers," the nuclear-powered submarines that carry the missiles that are designed to sea-launch into intercontinental ballistic orbit and strike anywhere on Earth that is named a target.

From his ultimate top insider's position, Butler had access to all the records we don't have as mere civilians. We frequently hear from those promoting a bigger military that we all have a duty to vote the Pentagon a *carte blanche*, an unlimited ticket, whatever they want, because they are the insiders, because they know what we can't. We the uniformed electorate can't know, we are told, because of national security. Butler ultimately told us that it is the other way around, too. This is part of what he meant when, in December 1995, he announced his opinion that nuclear weapons must be abolished; his point was dramatically underscored as he was joined by 60 more high-ranking military officers. It was indeed *because they knew what they were sworn not to reveal*: nuclear weapons have no humane, political or even military function. They are unusable, unstable, and they are dangerous even if never fired again. US American nuclear weapons have killed many Americans, not just "enemy" Japanese schoolchildren. These military men all knew what they couldn't tell us and what they could scarcely say out loud in the face of a giant *fait accompli*, an arsenal of tens of thousands of nuclear weapons poised, quivering, prepared to unleash annihilatory destruction well beyond whatever utility war may have ever had.

Examples of near-nuclear catastrophe are legion for all members of the nuclear club. In September 1980, a USAF B-52 bomber loaded with at least one thermonuclear weapon caught fire. Had the wind shifted, testified Dr. Roger Batzel to the Senate Appropriations Subcommittee on Defense in 1988, "You are talking about something that...could be probably worse than Chernobyl." (Earth: 15)

Other parts, some large and some small, of this huge story come out from time to time; even the most patriotic veterans occasionally rise above the orders dunned into them about secrecy, for they see, at long last, that the secrecy protects not the land we love, not the people of our families and communities and certainly not our most cherished freedoms. Military secrecy—especially when ordered to be carried on long past any conceivable need—is truly a tool to protect a model of global exploitation by threat and use of violence. Some call it the war system. This exploitation involves profiteering from the weapons systems manufacture *and* from the human and resource extraction made possible by coercion backed by those weapons. It is a wondrous system that manages to give the average worker in the dominant nation much more than the average worker in the dominated nations, thus buying loyalty couched in terms like "the American way," and "our guaranteed freedoms," or, "national interest."

This is what young Herb O'Brien believed as he entered the Korean War. O'Brien, from Finland, Minnesota, is just one of millions of vets who have been exposed to environmental dangers while serving in the military. Unlike the dangers of a glorious wound or death from hot flying steel, exposure to poison is universally regarded as an ignominious, pointless and pathetic death or debilitation. It is not even worth mentioning; it has no place in the pantheon of war stories. That is why O'Brien's story is emblematic of the untold numbers of vets who have been allowed to suffer—silently, for the most part—while we extol the brave soldiers and sailors who were killed or wounded in the fury of battle by the enemy's slashing weaponry. It is emotionally easier for a citizenry to hold high the hero hit by hot or cold steel than to be confronted with the Down's syndrome child of a vet who had been ordered to march toward a nuclear fireball. O'Brien's story is much more akin to those sad accounts of exuberant youth of England, France, Belgium, Russia and the United States during the trench warfare of World War 1 who were exposed to chemical attack and strangled to death or suffered terrible health until they died later. A horrified world outlawed such weaponry within seven years of the end of the war in which that weaponry was first introduced.

O'Brien was flying in a plane some 600 miles behind the lead plane in a practice run with nuclear bombs aboard both planes. The lead plane's bomb would be armed by radio signal and, presumably, when the bomb was away, both planes would turn back. But by a coincidence, the crystals in the radio receivers in both bombs were identical and the radio signal armed both bombs. O'Brien had to manually disarm the bomb in his plane, even though his "one-size-fits-all" suit didn't quite cover his throat area. "I'm a tall skinny guy," he said, "and I couldn't button my neck." (Simonson: A7)

Sworn to secrecy, O'Brien suffered various throat maladies without ever talking about what he felt was the probable cause—exposure to the high levels of radiation emanating from the early atomic weapons. He waited throughout the entire Cold War, dealing with his physical and emotional reactions in solitude. He waited until after he was diagnosed with throat cancer, ironically just as that very Cold War ended in 1990, when he lost his voice box to that very cancer. He finally brought it up in 1999, at last finding that the overriding need to expose it was of greater urgency than was continuing the charade of "loose lips sink ships" so-called security. In many, if not most, cases that intense secrecy has been a handy veil behind which the militaries of the world have operated with impunity and immunity since time immemorial. All these years later, O'Brien now says we ought to have negotiated a peace that avoided the Cold War.

It takes the Herb O'Briens as well as the General George Lee Butlers to break the military code of silence that subverts both democracy and ecology daily. The more of these outspoken vets we hear, the more we hear "the rest of the story." The earlier in their lives they find the bravery and wisdom to speak out—which requires much more cultural courage than does docilely heading off to war—the more profound their impacts will be, the more good they will do.

The immensity of the radiological war that has been waged against American lands and lifeways is staggering. It began with the mining of uranium in both the US and Canada, then proceeded through the milling, through the plutonium production and on through warhead fabrication. It has occurred at every transport step along the way, and in the testing of each nuclear weapon, whether above or below ground. It continues as these weapons are carried around the world, under the surface of the seas, and we have yet to dispose of a single bit of all of this safely.

From the Westinghouse-operated Idaho National Engineering Lab polluting the Rocky Mountains, to the Paducah Gaseous Diffusion plant run by Martin-Marietta exposing Kentuckians to atomic poison, from General Electric's nuclear handiwork at the Pinellas Plant in St. Petersburg, Florida, to Reynolds Electric's testing at Tonopah in Nye County, Nevada, the list of US corporate-run atomic operations that release radioactivity to our air, water and soil is long and revealing. (Cochran, et al.: 6)

> *Say the word defense and most people think of protection from an external threat: the danger of attack from another nation....*[O]*verlooked in the dynamics of the arms races – and their possible culmination in a nuclear holocaust – has been the comparatively less horrendous environmental consequences of making, assembling, transporting, and deploying modern weapons, including mining, refining, and processing the raw materials and disposing of the eventual wastes ... until recently ... abetted by the shroud of secrecy that has always surrounded matters of "national defense."*
>
> – Anne Ehrlich and John Birks (Ehrlich: vii)

This shroud is being lifted. It is the shroud of death for too many innocents, a cost of conflict that we have yet not properly counted.

trimmings from the Bomb: bury our mistakes

The last days of February 1986 were shocking ones. The DOE

> *(successor to the AEC) released nineteen thousand pages of documents on the history of the Hanford Site. From these, the public learned that radioactive and chemical wastes had been released far in excess of previously known levels.* (Gerber: 201)

Shortly after Wilhelm Roentgen created his X-ray machine in 1904, technicians began dying mysteriously. Exposure obviously caused radiation burns and skin ulcers, but further observation linked ionizing radiation to cancer, leukemia, degenerative diseases, congenital mental retardation, chromosomal damage and teratogenic defects. (Lenssen: 47)

The atomic waste left over from the production of bombs and from the nuclear reactors on-board ships and submarines amounts to a small percentage of the total nuclear waste in the US, most of which comes from commercial generation of electricity. (Lenssen: 46) Still, military waste is greater by volume, thanks to the virtually unregulated addition of erstwhile pure water to the bomb waste (*the solution to pollution is dilution*). The isotopes are just as deadly and long-lived. Plutonium remains deadly for its 24,400-year half-life, which means it continues its ionizing radiation emissions for a quarter-million years, only to degenerate completely into uranium-235, itself dangerous. Essentially, plutonium is forever, by human timescales.

And like the Midas Touch in reverse, everything near these weapons becomes itself radioactive over time. In the domes built over reactors, the radiation is so fierce it embrittles the reinforced concrete. When the military "disposes" of its old missile silos, however, it scatters all that radioactive concrete to the soil and winds.

> *Workers lace each silo with more than 800 pounds of dynamite, ammonia nitrate and fuel oil. The first explosion...sent chunks of concrete soaring 100 feet into the air... "People here are pretty trusting* [says a local woman]*...If the government tells you it's going to be all right, you believe them. I don't know if that's trusting or naive..." most likely, the land used for missile sites will be sold for farmland, said Staff Sgt. Rob Mims.* (Johnson: 4A)

Anyone who has ever visited the silo sites in question knows that many of them have corn or other crops growing right up to the fencelines, depending on which state and which missile field we consider.

In fact, the US nuclear weapons reservation at Hanford, Washington has released at least double the total radiation which blasted out of the USSR's Chernobyl reactors in 1986. (INFACT: 15) Contractor GE continues to attempt to make the US taxpayer foot the near-impossible clean-up, though the contractor was certainly prepared to take all the short term profits. It's not unlike the various financing schemes by which the American taxpayers ponied up for the transcontinental railroads in the 1870s—only to have private rail barons take the profits and turn to the government when initial shoddy construction required massive reconstruction. For every colossal mistake made by war profiteers they have a plan for a tremendously expensive clean-up. It is not only profitable on both ends for the elite owners, but all of it gets added to the nation's GNP, despite the lugubrious note that none of it all could ever be used to elevate the human condition, and that, to the contrary, it has continued to worsen it. Like an obese patient, the economy of a nation that has spent more than $5 trillion on nuclear weapons is not necessarily healthier because it has more fat. It is flirting with an economic cardiac "event" and an ecological event concomitantly.

Depleted uranium: war with nuclear waste

> *The United Sates has conducted two nuclear wars. The first against Japan in 1945, the second in Kuwait and Iraq in 1991.*
>
> —Dr. Helen Caldicott, Australian physician, founder of both Physicians for Social Responsibility and Women's Action for Nuclear Disarmament (Caldicott: 18)

The Pentagon has more than a billion pounds of nuclear waste (Atoms: 15); it has no geologically safe method nor any politically acceptable method of "disposing" of that poisonous garbage—so it's giving it away to industry in the form of depleted uranium. And it's giving away cancer. This, from the US Army Armament, Munitions and Chemical Command in July, 1990, stating that DU is a: "low level alpha radiation emitter which is linked to cancer when exposures are internal, [and] chemical toxicity causing kidney damage." (Fahey: i)

The war industries are then, in turn, using the depleted uranium to make anti-tank shells, superdense and pyrophoric, kinetically and thermally cutting through hardened steel cladding and roasting those sad souls on the inside of ill-fated tanks. While a gallon of water, for example, weighs eight pounds, a single gallon of DU tips in at the average adult male weights of 152 pounds. (Atoms: 15) Alloyed with two percent molybdenum for hardness, these shells are also fired in tests, to litter the landscape and seabeds from the now-abandoned base in Panama, the Puerto Rican island of Vieques and ranges in the western deserts, Michigan, Kansas, Maryland and Indiana. When, for example, an engine fire ignited a stockpile of DU weapons, the entire remains were buried in the nuclear waste dump in South Carolina. (Atoms: 15) That depleted uranium has now been used in at least two wars (to add one, then, to Caldicott's list of nuclear wars), shot from US Thunderbolt A-10 Wart Hog war planes.

DU was used in the 1991 Gulf War. According to the Iraqi government, children still find shiny, silvery pieces of the shells and children still contract radiation-induced sickness from those pieces of DU shells. The extent of the causal link has not yet been established to the satisfaction of most independent health analysts, partially because of the ongoing sanctions and partly because of natural Pentagon resistance to the other population making claims about health effects of DU, combat veterans. We hear, on the one hand, horrifying statistics and ghastly anecdotal claims from the Iraqi government and some veterans, and, on the other, the Pentagon cavalierly dismissing any DU danger whatsoever. (Center, 1999: 1) We are in the early stages of a debate and, once again, society seems incapable of reigning in the sheer size of this experiment, which may make it a very large and unnecessary risk.

In Yugoslavia, during the 1999 78-day air attack, "depleted uranium from 30 mm armor-piercing rounds fired by A-10 Wart Hog planes drifted invisibly through the air. An initial investigation by the United Nations and the Swedish Radiation Institute found no dangerous radioactivity from weapons containing depleted uranium. NATO and the Pentagon have also downplayed such health risks during the conflict. For years, US veterans groups have said that depleted uranium caused cancer and other illnesses after its use in munitions during the 1991 Persian Gulf war." (Fleishman) It has not helped matters that Saddam Hussein has not allowed the World Health Organization into Iraq to properly examine the question. Nor has it helped researchers that the Pentagon refused for more than a year to say where DU was used in the Yugoslavian air attack. (Center, 1999: 1)

While the Pentagon gives away DU literally for free, the war profiteering corporations, including Remington, Honeywell, Olin, Aerojet Heavy Metals and Nuclear Metals have then used this free DU to make profits in resale back to the Pentagon. (Atoms: 15)

Where have these radioactive shells been produced, stored and tested? The Pentagon isn't providing an overall picture. Each bit of information must be dredged up, usually by independent investigative journalists or environmentalists. We know, for example, that in February 1999 a Marine aircraft fired DU shells during training at the Navy's Vieques Island bombing range in Puerto Rico. Only 57 of the 263 shells were recovered. The navy admits the training violated both the Nuclear Regulatory Commission and official navy training practices. (Center, 1999: 1) The transparency of the Clinton administration has applied far more to its examination of the mistakes of past regimes even as it engages in its own cover-ups of DU use.

in the interest of spacy science

On 17 October 1997 the National Aeronautics and Space Administration launched the controversial Cassini space probe carrying 72.3 lbs. of plutonium, the most lethal substance ever created by humans. NASA's own Environmental Impact Statement warned that, if the probe accidentally reëntered the Earth's atmosphere as it "swung by" in August 1999 following its loop around Venus in June, about "5 billion" people on Earth would be exposed to airborne plutonium, one speck of which could result in lethal lung cancer. (Altenberg) While there was no atmospheric catastrophe, environmentalists raised the philosophical, practical question, "What benefit, what risk?"

Journalist and journalism professor Karl Grossman of State University of New York/College at Old Westbury, has uncovered much of the Pentagon agenda and reported it in *The Progressive*, *U.S. News & World Report*, *The Nation*, and in his book, ***The Wrong Stuff: The Space Program's Nuclear Threat to Our Planet***. Grossman cites the Pentagon's own literature, a 1996 report titled *Vision For 2020*:

> *US Space Command – dominating the space dimension of military operations to protect US interests and investment. Integrating Space Forces into warfighting capabilities across the full spectrum of conflict.* (Grossman, 2000: 1)

On the chance that readers did not fully apprehend the import of proclaiming space in the name of US investment, the Pentagon report gets definitive: "The globalization of the world economy will also continue, with a widening between the 'haves' and 'have-nots.' (Grossman, 2000: 2) This sounds like lefty rhetoric from the Battle of Seattle or the A-16 DC debacle, but it is what in fact highlights the concerns of those who eventually took to the streets in the name of fighting a kind of globalization of greed. Few knew that the US Space Command was preparing to defend this kind of globalization; likely few would be surprised. That the Space Command proudly points to its suppliers from the corporate world—some 75 major weaponeers, from Boeing to TRW—only introduces one more reinforcing fastener in this brand of globalization. (Grossman, 1999: 8)

The nuclear-powered space-fighting platforms will generally fight with lasers, but any weapon is itself a target. When will the first plutonium-powered warfighting spacecraft be blown apart to send its disintegrated poisons dispersing into the lofts of the the high atmosphere?

Comprehensive Test Ban Treaty: betrayal as usual

The Partial Test Ban Treaty was signed in August of 1963 by Kennedy and Khruschev and, right on cue, the peace movement rolled over and played dead. We are still waiting for the rest of the story, the other shoe to drop, for the Comprehensive Test Ban Treaty to be signed by the largest remaining nuclear power on the planet, the United States. The defeat in the US Senate in October 1999 of this crucial step for humanity hobbles all other efforts to disarm nuclear weapons.

Prevailing wisdom suggests that Republican retribution against Bill Clinton seems to have been at the core of the successful effort to bury the treaty as deeply as the underground blast caverns in Nevada. And global reaction to this defeat was swift and vociferous. Russia, China, Singapore, Germany, Japan, England, France and many more nations spoke out strongly and immediately, deploring the US failure to ratify. "The perception here is one of disbelief," said Andrew Brooks, a defense analyst at London's International Institute for Strategic Studies. "This is the chance for the biggest superpower to freeze the nuclear mechanisms, and [it is] behaving like a small child." (News Services: B1)

It has been the failure of the US to sign the Comprehensive Test Ban Treaty that has been blamed for the reactive failure of the Russian Duma to ratify START 2, though that has now been done under Russia's new president, that well-known peacenik, Vladimir Putin. Perhaps that will reverse the negative effects of the various treaty imbroglios. Perhaps we will revisit the CTBT in time to reverse the nuclear arms race on the subcontinent, where India and Pakistan used the US/UK/Russia/France/China arms control failures to justify breaking out of what they call "nuclear apartheid."

Indeed, the only way to stop the inevitable descent into the massive malappropriation of resources into this toxic technology is to take bold, unilateral steps. If the nation-states together cannot manage it, individual nation-states must. If they also fail, the people will eventually do the job themselves and the "leaders" will follow, as with the landmine treaty.

sources

Altenburg, Patricia, "Stop the Cassini Earth Flyby," Grandmothers for Peace research brochure, 1999.

Atoms & Waste, "The Pentagon's Nuclear Ammo," *Earth Island Journal*, Fall 1991: 15.

Butler, General George Lee, "Ending the Nuclear Madness," Waging Peace Series #40. Santa Barbara CA: Nuclear Age Peace Foundation, 1999.

Caldicott, Dr. Helen, "A New Kind of Nuclear War," in John Catalinotto and Sara Flounders, editors, ***Metal of Dishonor, Depleted Uranium: How the***

Pentagon Radiates Soldiers and Civilians with DU Weapons. NYC: International Action Center, 1999 (original 1997).

Catalinotto, John, and Sara Flounders, editors, ***Metal of Dishonor, Depleted Uranium: How the Pentagon Radiates Soldiers and Civilians with DU Weapons***. NYC: International Action Center, 1999 (original 1997).

Center for Defense Information, "Depleted Uranium—a necessary evil?," The Defense Monitor, XXVIII:6, 1999: 1-4.

Center for Defense Information, ***1997 CDI Military Almanac***. Washington DC: Center for Defense Information, 1997.

Coyle, Dana, et al., ***Deadly Defense: Military Radioactive Landfills***. NYC: Radioactive Waste Campaign, 1988.

Earth Island Journal, "A 'Near Chernobyl' in North Dakota," Fall 1991: 15.

Ehrlich, Anne H and John W. Birks, editors, ***Hidden Dangers: Environmental Consequences of Preparing for War***. San Francisco: Sierra Club Books, 1990.

Ellsberg, Daniel, lecture workshop, 1985, St. Louis, Missouri Nuclear Freeze conference.

Gerber, Michele Stenehjem, ***On the Home Front: The Cold War Legacy of the Hanford Nuclear Site***. Lincoln NE: University of Nebraska Press, 1992.

Grossman, Karl, "Waging War in Space," *The Nation*, 27 December 1999: 8.

Grossman, Karl, presentation, University of Texas-Austin, PSA/COPRED conference, 1 April 2000.

Fahey, Dan, ***Depleted Uranium Exposures: Case Narrative***, 3rd edition. San Francisco: Swords to Plowshares, 1998.

Johnson, Dirk, "Cold War relics are blasted to bits," *St. Paul Pioneer Press*, 19 October 1999.

Lenssen, Nicholas, "Confronting Nuclear Waste," ***State of the World 1992***. New York: W.W. Norton & Co., 1992.

Longley, Robert, "Hanford Site: Past Horror, Future Hope." http://usgovinfo.com/library/weekly/aa102497.htm , 8 March 1999.

Mason, Bobbie Ann, "Fallout: Paducah's secret nuclear disaster," *The New Yorker,* 10 January 2000: 30-36.

New Services, "World dismayed by treaty vote," *Minneapolis Star-Tribune*, 15 October 1999: 1B.

Simonson, Jennifer, "Herb O'Brien helped disarm a hydrogen bomb," *Budgeteer News*, 7 November 1999: A7.

White, Jonathan R., ***Terrorism: An Introduction***. 2nd edition. New York: West/Wadsworth Publishing, 1998.

Conventional biochem surprise: attacking from within

biophobic bioterrorists: are they aliens?

When a mosquito-borne virus began to kill New Yorkers by literally feverishly cooking their brains in August 1999, the Centers for Disease Control lab in Colorado and the Emerging Diseases Lab at UC-Irvine simultaneously discovered by pathological examination of brain tissue from the dead New Yorkers that it was a new virus closely related to the Ugandan West Nile virus and its close cousin, Australian Kunjin virus. (Preston: 92)

Hello, biophobia. The NYC mayor's office reacted much as Lewis Thomas described the response by the human immune system to foreign elements in the bloodstream: attack with everything we have, even if it makes us sick. Helicopters sprayed insecticides all over the city and many suburbs. The mayor's chief of Emergency Management, Jerome Hauer, cornered the market on the biotoxic spray, Off! with a purchase of five million cans. The long-range effects of the "cure" may kill as many as the "outbreak." Seven died and approximately 50 were taken ill from the virus; reliable statistics are not available to predict how many will contract cancer and die from the poisons in the insecticides. The CIA investigated on the chance that some agents of Saddam or Sudan or other nefarious foreign elements were responsible for this bioterroristic attack.

There were uneasy connections. A writer claiming to be an Iraqi defector with experience as a Saddam double (assassination foil tactic) had been published months before with an account of one of his final meetings with Saddam, during which the Iraqi leader had supposedly claimed to now control a bioweapon containing a strain of *West Nile virus.* (Preston: 105)

Saddam and his agents? A CIA-engineered plot to justify their own existence and the existence of sanctions? We don't know. What we do know is that this kind of tension and this kind of fear of the natural is the sad and predictable result of a military model of conflict management rapidly losing any evolutionary adaptiveness it may have ever had.

Saddam was, after all, a long-term client and protégé of the Soviet Union and it was there, in what is now the Crimea, that the first documented cases of biological warfare occurred. In the 14th century, Tartars catapulted plague-ridden corpses over the walls, beginning the phenomenon of warfare intentionally literally launching contagious disease. (Alibek: 166)

According to the official who oversaw the Soviet biological warfare program, and who defected to the US in 1992, the elaborate treaty-cheating practiced by the Soviet Union was emulated by Saddam. (Alibek: 140) In fact, the Soviet Union, which had the largest covert bioweapon program anywhere, spent "decades building institutes and training scientists in India, Iraq, and Iran" as well as "Eastern Europe, Cuba, Libya" and others. The biological weapons programs in those countries have often hired former Soviet bioweaponeers. Kanatjan "Ken" Alibek has little doubt that, as late as 1995, Iraq was still purchasing major biological warfare equipment. (Alibek: 275)

When the object is to kill people in order to gain power, morality is not a consideration. Stabbing and shooting and bombing are so drastic that the purveyors of death can hardly be expected to ignore any possible weapon or method of killing. Sir Arthur "Bomber" Harris put it best when he was challenged regarding his decision to bomb Dresden, Cologne, Hamburg and other German cities during World War II: "Stabbing a man with a bayonet is wrong. Show me one act of war that is moral." (Ringler) Iraq's biowarfare capabilities, like those of any modern military, were justified with rhetoric about deterrence and the need for antidote development, in case enemy militaries attacked with such low-down weapons. Thus the Iraqis hired the French company Institut Merieux to build them a facility toward that end in the early 1980s, the Al Manal plant, where, for example, 20,000 liters of the highly lethal botulinum toxin—BTX—were produced during the Gulf War. While a portion of that site was demolished at the behest of UNSCOM inspectors in 1992, those inspectors have been booted out of Iraq since 1997 and the bioweaponry may be back in production now. (Preston: 105) It must be faced: all the reprobative censure heaped upon Saddam Hussein and his ilk has little effect if the US maintains bioweapon production capability of its own. From the Dugway Proving Grounds to the major lab facility at Reston, Virginia, the US continues to research biological weaponry. Like Baghdad or Moscow, Washington claims it is all in the interest of preparing antidotes.

In a way, the history of biological weaponry has been a template for the development and subsequent disarmament attempts for chemical, and then atomic, weaponry. Following the horrific use of asphyxiating gasses and the extreme fear of germ warfare following World War 1, the responsible nations of the world developed and signed the 17 June 1925

Geneva Protocol, which outlawed the actual use in warfare of such agents. The US signed on after thinking it over for half a century, on 22 January 1975. But the real treaty, the one that outlawed the biological weaponry itself, and therefore the development and mere possession of any of it, wasn't negotiated to successful conclusion until 10 April 1972, and 157 nations now agree that no biological arsenal research, development, production, possession or use is legal. (Center, 1997: 49)

That gap, that long failure to actually outlaw biological research, produced a protracted terrorism that persists, and with regrettably excellent reason. Research into organisms that produce horrifying death to humans has gone on apace around the world and we have come closer than we wish to think to experiencing outbreaks of virulent cataclysms. Recently declassified US, Canadian, Chinese and North Korean documents reveal programs of pan-homicidally lethal arsenals. (Endicott: *ix*) A recent set of revelations from a defected former Soviet Union biological weaponeer tell a similar tale of state terrorism in that monstrous arsenal. (Alibek: *x*) Under the excuse of antidote preparation, major biological covert programs have been building huge stockpiles of anthropathogens: strains of anthrax, tularemia, Q fever, brucellosis, glanders and other literal plagues. Disease control experts watch warily as the occasional sick worker leaves such a "defensive" facility, perhaps with a sniffle, a cough, a little fever. Will this be the escape of ebola into rural Virginia and will it run amok through the Eastern seaboard? It has come perilously close to happening and it will not be until these facilities are seriously, totally shut down and dismantled that we will attain a greater measure of safety. As ever, our increased security comes not through more weapons research but through a bigger investment in methods of promoting peaceful solutions.

Better dying through chemicals

The nation-states are the biggest, most dispassionate producers and purveyors of chemical weaponry, but it is indeed odd that so few small-time terrorist organizations have chosen those means, since non-nuclear weapons of mass destruction are vastly cheaper and easier to produce and deliver. One of those few, the Aum Shinrikyo sect, carved out new morally low ground for the NGO sector in their attempt to seize power from the Japanese government by synchronous release of five canisters of sarin gas. They employed this deadly odorless chemical agent in an attack on the subway system in Tokyo on 20 March 1995, which killed 12 and sent 5,500 to the hospital. (White: 233)

This is one of many sections of this book that could pose the perspective query: Who are the terrorists? What governments are guilty of state-sponsored terrorism? Governments that dwell in glass domes ought not launch explosive charges.

The US alone has tens of thousands of chemical munitions, stored now on the Johnston Atoll near Hawaii and in eight army depots across the US from Oregon to Maryland. Choking gas, blood gas, blister gas, nerve gas and other demonic matériels are in line for destruction and disposal, though the methods themselves are potential catastrophes. (Birks: 164, 168, 172) Since the Chemical Weapons Convention entered into force 29 April 1997 it has not merely been immoral to possess these hellish devices, it has been illegal. 169 nations agree in signature, 125 by ratification. (Center, 1999: 54) Now, when the incineration of VX nerve gas introduces elements to the atmosphere, it will be done in keeping with the new law, but if elements leak onto the soil of a military base, it will be illegal. As ever, both will be toxic to life.

electromagnetic radiation (EMR)

In 1958, physicist Nicolos Cristofilos predicted that one of the results from a nuclear explosion would be an electromagnetic impulse. This EMP could disrupt much of the nearby electronic activity, he said, and therefore knock out communication to the nuclear forces just when it was needed most. He then also posited an unjammable form of electronic signal, extremely low frequency waves. The ELF wave would be huge, some 2,500 miles long, and thus would be impervious to the effects of localized explosions.

Cristofilos was proven correct concerning the EMP when an open-air nuclear test in the South Pacific did indeed black out portions of Hawaii and other adjacent areas. The navy set to work to develop ELF, its emergency command band of communication in the event of nuclear attack. Numerous possible signal generation configurations were proposed, including ELF balloons, ELF trucks and, the most massive of all, Project Sanguine.

Sanguine would have consisted of approximately 6,000 miles of buried antenna cable, powered by one or more "slave" nuclear power plants. All of this would have been hardened against nuclear attack, buried deep—sealed and steeled concretely, literally. This plan settled on the Laurentian Shield bedrock of northern Wisconsin and, once announced, was met with instant statewide opposition in the late 1960s.

The navy eventually backed down and proposed Project Seafarer, a somewhat scaled-back proposal. Seafarer was going to be 2,500 miles of cable and it was proposed for Michigan. The reception there was no warmer and, during the Environmental Impact Statement process, then-president Jimmy Carter promised then-governor of Michigan, Warren Milliken, that "Seafarer will never be built against the wishes of the

Michigan people."

To borrow from the country song, "Never didn't last that long." Though approximately 80 percent of the voters in the Upper Peninsula of Michigan voted against the ELF installation in referenda in every U.P. county, the next president, Ronald Reagan, reversed the Carter promise and, in 1981, ordered ELF built in Michigan and "upgraded" in Wisconsin.

Back in 1969, during the bitter battle to defeat Sanguine ELF in Wisconsin, the navy built the Wisconsin Test Facility, a down-sized version of the mega-system publicly proposed. In the atmosphere of citizen opposition, the navy promised in a press release on 1 April 1969 that the WTF would be "dismantled and removed from the national forest once testing is completed."

April Fools. That facility is still in Wisconsin and testing is complete; it was linked to the Michigan ELF system and sends commands, one-way, to all nuclear-powered submarines under US command, including the Trident fleet and all fast-attack and all hunter-killer submarines. It currently even relays signals to British nuclear subs.

The electromagnetic radiation that emanates from ELF is suspected to promote cellular growth. In navy testing, it showed increased weight gain in male adolescent primates. It is suspected to cause cell growth generally, which, in the case of cancer, is a decidedly negative manifestation. Southern Ashland County, Wisconsin, where the WTF has been generating ELF for more than three decades, shows a strong cluster of cancers. "Regional data provided by National Cancer Center indicates that the Northern Wisconsin Economic Area was ranked in the top 10 % for cancer deaths involving white females from 1950 to 1969 for esophagus and stomach cancers, and leukemia." (Lac Courte Oreilles: 28)

Naturally, there is no way to prove the connection, other than common-sense epidemiology. Still, when the EIS was challenged in federal court in 1983, the federal judge ruled that ELF upgrading underway in Wisconsin and construction then underway in Michigan must be halted until the human health questions could be more adequately addressed. The navy applied pressure and the appellate panel in Chicago issued a two-sentence expedited verbal ruling lifting the construction injunction on the grounds of "national security." The health issues have never been revisited, and ELF runs 24-7, though the Cold War has been declared won and done. In a 1997 DoD-sponsored report carefully titled ***An Evaluation of the U.S. Navy's Extremely Low Frequency Communications System Ecological Monitoring Program***, the National Research Council reported on: the grant proposals, on the grants themselves, on the reports from the Illinois Institute of Technology contract on monitoring ELF *but not on the human health effects*. This area was specifically occluded from the Council's brief. (National: ix)

Meanwhile, in Alaska, the Pentagon has funded and begun another "test" technology with yet another innocuous sounding name, the high-frequency active auroral research program, or HAARP. Its purpose is unclear, since its application could potentially manipulate weather, alter or eliminate electronic communications, or produce neurological effects. (Begich: 9) The tool is a generation device using approximately 1.7 gigawatts (billion watts) of electricity (Begich: 8) to hammer the ionosphere, dwarfing the 1.25 million watts thrumming through the Wisconsin ELF lines. While the kneejerk reaction of the military is to experiment on the chance that a new technology could have fighting application, the citizen response, increasingly, is to resist first. There is just too much evidence that the armed forces are perpetually prepared to conduct huge experiments using life itself as a giant guinea pig. HAARP is certainly one of those suspicious electromagnetic projects.

General Operations: he's a five-star hazard

On 3 February 1998, in a peaceful valley near Cavalese in the Dolomite Mountains of the Italian Alps, US Marine Corps pilot Richard Ashby flew his jet much lower than regulations allowed. It remains unclear whether he was simply mistaken or whether he was "Top Gun hot-dogging" for the benefit of a ski resort full of tourists, a long-standing complaint of local residents. Ashby admitted pocketing the routine videotape of the flight and claimed it was somehow lost. In the end, that was the only charge that stuck, and he was sentenced to six months for destroying what may have been clear evidence that he was guilty of manslaughter. The military prosecutor and the military jury managed to slip Ashby that elite club's golden parachute through lackluster evidentiary and lenient rulings. For example, incredibly, the military prosecutor never asked Ashby whether the usual altitude alarm had sounded when the war plane descended below the 1,000-feet regulatory minimum. (Thompson: 3A)

At about 300 feet off the ground, his EA-6B Prowler wing sliced through a steel cable, literally the lifeline for vacationing skiers riding in a gondola. The 20 Europeans must have died in horrific terror following that long, tumbling plunge. On 3 March 1999 Ashby was acquitted by an eight-Marine Corps jury of 20 counts, including manslaughter. The verdict precipitated "joyous whoops" from his friends and relatives and outrage from relatives of those killed, many of whom attended the Camp LeJune, North Carolina trial. "I buried my husband a year ago," said Rita Wunderlich, whose husband, Jurgen, was in the gondola. "Today was his second funeral." (Vogel: 6A) Italian Prime Minister Massimo D'Alema, visiting in the US, said he and the Italian people were "shocked and baffled" that no one was held responsible for this "massacre." (Simon:

3A) D'Alema made no call to close the NATO air base at Aviano in northern Italy, which was about to be one of the busiest launch points during the Kosovo-Serbia air attack that would be initiated some three weeks after the acquittal.

Accidents happen. On 8 April 2000, a Marine Corps MV-22 Osprey, a war plane touted as being capable of helicopter take off and turboprop cruise, suddenly plunged into the ground at a small airport in Marana, Arizona, exploding and killing all 19 Marines on board. It was the third such Osprey incident in the last decade. (Schmitt: 1A) Routine military operations—like any human endeavor—result in mistakes. It could happen to anyone; routine spills, leaks, dumps and accidents are commonplace in the military. Some would assert that these regrettable practices are, or have been, more common there than in other sectors of human activity because society tends to look the other way. We are not supposed to pry into the warriors' preparations to defend us, after all. Only spies and traitors do that.

That is indeed the reticence the militaries of the world would prefer that the citizens, the politicians and the media assume when approaching the military, gingerly, respectfully, hesitantly. Sadly, the militaries generally have done little to deserve the secrecy afforded their routine operations and much to militate for close inspection. More Superfund sites are associated with the DoD and its attendant industries than any other agency or economic sector. Stories about generally wasteful and environmentally harmful activities are commonplace.

I was talking to a class at a Minnesota University about the hidden costs of militarism in the fall of 1996 and a young fellow stayed afterward to tell me that, when he was on active duty just the year before, he was ordered to dump about 20,000 gallons of jet fuel overboard, as the navy was nearing the end of its fiscal year and needed to use up its reserves or face budget cutbacks. "Pilots were up in the air constantly," he told me, "not even doing real training, just burning fuel, but they couldn't go through it all, so they told us to dump it." Summoning his courage, this young man refused, but the next crew on duty simply did the job. Will we ever know how often this happens? Will we ever count this cost to the oceans?

The technology of killing requires practice, and deaths from practicing to kill are particularly ironic. If it happens to a military personnel, it is a bathetic twist, all part of a high-risk job, a karmic catastrophe. But when it happens to civilians, it is objectionable. With protectors like these, quite seriously, who needs enemies? And when it happens to civilian nationals of other nations who happen to live or work near or on US forward bases in Italy, Germany, Okinawa, or anywhere, it can register as severely unjust.

Thus, when, in April 1999, an errant bombing run on the Puerto Rican island of Vieques killed a Puerto Rican civilian security guard, the Puerto Rican populace and their friends reacted. Citizens began to camp on the bombing range in resistance to any further such training. In a frank admission of a part of the problem—the island has been attacked by many kinds of US weapons, including depleted uranium shells—US Senate candidate (and US First Lady) Hillary Rodham Clinton, in a written statement in October 1999, said, "There should be an immediate and permanent end to the bombing. Use of live fire on the island has put the people of Vieques at risk, degraded the environment and hampered economic development." Meanwhile, the Clinton White House panel recommended continuing the bombing while the president lamented that the people of Puerto Rico "feel estranged" from the military. (Burns: 3A)

As we learn of the contamination of our food, air and water by shoddy practices of the militaries, feeling estranged begins to feel normal.

sources

Alibek, Ken, ***Biohazard: The Chilling True Story of the Largest Covert Biological Weapons Program in the World—Told from the Inside by the Man Who Ran It***. NYC: Random House, 1999.

Altenburg, Patricia, "Stop the Cassini Earth Flyby," Grandmothers for Peace research brochure, 1999.

Begich, Dr. Nick and Jeane Manning, ***Angels Don't Play This HAARP: Advances in Tesla Technology***. Anchorage AK: 1995.

Birks, John, "Weapons Forsworn: Chemical and Biological Weapons," in Anne H. Ehrlich and John W. Birks, editors, ***Hidden Dangers: Environmental Consequences of Preparing for War***. San Francisco: Sierra Club Books, 1990.

Burns, Robert, "White House panel says practice bombing on island should go on," *Duluth News-Tribune*, Associated Press, 19 October 1999: 3A.

Center for Defense Information, ***1997 CDI Military Almanac***. Washington DC: Center for Defense Information, 1997.

Center for Defense Information, ***1999 CDI Military Almanac***. Washington DC: Center for Defense Information, 1999.

Earth Island Journal, "A 'Near Chernobyl' in North Dakota," Fall 1991: 15.

Endicott, Stephen and Edward Hagerman, ***The Unites States and Biological Warfare: Secrets from the Early Cold War and Korea***. Bloomington IN: Indiana University Press, 1998.

Fleishman, Jeffery, "Yugoslavia is afloat in 'war waste,'" *The Philadelphia Inquirer*, 14 October 1999.

Lac Courte Oreilles Tribe, ***Mitigation Plan of the Lac Courte Oreilles Indian Tribe of Wisconsin Concerning the U.S. Navy's Project ELF***. Hayward WI: Lac Courte Oreilles Tribe, 2000.

Longley, Robert, "Hanford Site: Past Horror, Future Hope." http://usgovinfo.com/library/weekly/aa102497.htm , 8 March 1999.

National Research Council, ***An Evaluation of the U.S. Navy's Extremely Low Frequency Communications System Ecological Monitoring Program***. Washington DC: National Academy Press, 1997.

Preston, Richard, "West Nile Mystery," *The New Yorker*, 18 October 1999: 89-108.

Ringler, Dick, "Dilemmas of War and Peace" audiotape. Madison WI: University of Wisconsin, 1993.

Schmitt, Eric, "Crash kill 19 Marines, renewing questions," *Duluth News-Tribune*, *New York Times*, 10 April 2000: 1A+.

Simon, Roger, "Italy's D'Alema unswayed by Clinton apology," *Duluth News-Tribune*, *Chicago Tribune*, 6 March 1999: 3A

Thompson, Estes, "Pilot in gondola crash says he was engrossed in map," *Duluth News-Tribune*, Associated Press, 27 February 1999: 3A.

United States Coast Guard, "Coast Guard enforces federal pollution laws to protect Lake Superior," *Budgeteer News*, 7 March 1999: B5.

Vogel, Steve, "Marine acquitted in cable car deaths," *Duluth News-Tribune*, *Washington Post*, 5 March 1999: 1A, 6A.

White, Jonathan R., ***Terrorism: An Introduction***. 2nd edition. New York: West/ Wadsworth Publishing, 1998.

Arms racism: the militaries' attack on indigenous lands and lifeways

> *Whitefeather of the Ojibway, grandson of Loonsfoot and Red Bird Woman,*
>
> *In the name of the Native American People:*
>
> *I ask the government of the United States of America, so-called by the great-great grandchildren of immigrants who came to my land 492 winters past, to take from our Mother the Earth these machines of fire that destroy earth and human life throughout the lands of all people. I act today, as the Old Ones have said I must, to take our stand, to make our land calm once again.*
>
> *The trees must remain green, the waters must be crystal, the sands are to be pure and warm once again.*
>
> *The sage and sweet grass, where the deer and elk lay their heads, must once more be safe and soft for them. Where the children shall walk and grow must be peaceful and warm; no bad shall they hear, and only good things their eyes shall see.*
>
> *The circle we form which knows no color and knows no end, as our feet touch our Mother the Earth, shall not feel the hurt and destruction of fire.*
>
> *The winds are pure, and the Grandfathers have told us the time is now when peace must come from the North Wind, where the Old Ones have gone and only they, with the Great Spirit, know what is tomorrow.*
>
> —Larry Cloud Morgan (Whitefeather), White Earth/Cass Lake Ojibway

The above was written by Whitefeather before traveling to the nuclear missile fields of Missouri with two Catholic priests, a mother of seven developmentally disabled foster children and a set of hammers to begin very personally dismantling the live, locked and loaded nuclear arsenal of the United States on 11 November 1984, Armistice Day. (Morgan: 2) For this, Whitefeather was sentenced to eight years in prison. During that time his diabetes worsened and, in early summer of 1999, he walked on to the spirit world.

Larry Cloud Morgan was an artist, a poet, a playwright and a language preservationist. He was a McKnight Fellow and won several other human service awards. He was on the Board of Directors of many peace and justice organizations and was a co-founder of Justice Camp at White Earth Ojibwe reservation. Ironically, his frequent partner in the defense of the rights of Native peoples at White Earth was former US federal judge Miles Lord. They met on the federal plane that was transporting Cloud Morgan to prison, where the jurist apologized to Whitefeather for the unprecedented harshness of a fellow district judge toward Whitefeather and the other nonviolent resisters. Later, after Cloud Morgan was out of prison and Lord retired from the bench, the elderly judge often drove the disabled Native Holy Man to ceremonies and political events at White Earth reservation, in northwestern Minnesota. Cloud Morgan also traveled to Scotland to witness against the British Trident and to Florida to lead prayers for disarmament of the new US Trident base at Kings Bay, Georgia. For this act he knew he would be violated (prisoner parlance for "arrested for a violation of the conditions of parole" or probation) and sent back to prison, which he was. Larry Cloud Morgan was also a participant in many spiritual activities domestically and abroad. He also led many interfaith ceremonies, including one unique mass at the Cathedral of St. Paul in St. Paul, Minnesota, where he conducted the rituals partly in traditional Catholic fashion and partly in traditional Native American fashion. Larry dedicated his life to saving the Earth, saving his people and resisting evil nonviolently. As a boy, he told his large family at the dinner table, "I cannot go the way of my older brothers into the military." His grandfather thought about it and said, "Good. Larry has his own way."

confluence of problems, coalition of protest

When a military of a nation-state damages indigenous lands and lifeways, several issues arise around which there are citizen groups or movements: militarism, Native rights, and environmental harms. Larry Cloud Morgan was a treaty rights activist and a nonviolent resister to militarism. His environmentalism expressed itself in his embrace of Native lifeways. His integrity and integration combined in a rare synthesis, attributes lending themselves to a more complex, holistic analysis.

Political scientists refer to groups of activists as "public interest groups, citizen groups, single-interest groups, cause groups, eternality groups, alternative groups or expressive interest groups." (Libby: 1, 5) Clearly, this category includes environmental groups, disarmament groups, peace groups and Native rights groups. These organizations have, at times, worked in coalition with tribal governments or consortia of tribal councils, at which point their power and access to both media and the law jumps dramatically. But the coalitions are rare and so are successes. Part of this lack of unity is cultural confusion and part is a lack of a synoptic viewpoint, a failure to appreciate a meta-analysis of the confluence of peace, Native American and environmental issues. Coalition can work to help the struggles of all three movements. It is critical to continue to raise questions of the sacrifices versus the gains of such coalitional work. Dr. Bernice Johnson Reagon said it best: "If you're comfortable in your coalition, it's not broad enough."

> *Our land is suffering on account of nuclear testing and uranium mining. We have to preserve this Earth. We rely on this Earth to give us food, clothing, and all the luxury that we have. Everything is here for us to use, but nuclear energy is not the way to continue with what we have.*
>
> —Corbin Harney, Western Shoshone Spiritual Leader (Harney: frontispiece)

When Corbin Harney writes of being reliant upon the land for food and clothing and even luxury, is he referring to DVDs and SUVs? I don't think so; he is a spiritual leader who is focused on preserving and restoring the indigenous economy, which, according to Winona LaDuke and others, is simply not compatible with an extractive, war-driven, European-style economy. Indeed, the very roots of the common Judeo-Christian approach to the human-Earth relationship are antithetical to much of what we hear from Native philosophy. There is no Cartesian duality, no hierarchy of human over Earth, no real analog to the best of the Judeo-Christian biblical stewardship ethic or the worst of the extractive ethos. Protection of a common heritage is the default setting, so to speak, for most Native cultures; protection of private property is the norm evoked in the Judeo-Christian ethic. In its most extreme distortion, the military serves to guard and perpetuate this latter ethic unto destruction.

> *They are acting in service to the fundamental principle that has informed technical evolution in the modern era: If it can be done, do it. There are no boundaries, no rules, no sets of standards by which to moderate these activities....The assumptions have been gaining strength for thousands of years, fed ... by Judeo-Christian religious doctrines that have de-sanctified the earth and place humans in domination over it....we have lost a sense of the sacredness of the natural world.*
>
> —Jerry Mander (Mander: 187)

When Dr. Robert Brander organized a conference of Native Medicine Lodge leaders some years ago at the Sigurd Olson Environmental Institute in Ashland, Wisconsin, the stories were all similar; the medicine people were traveling farther from home to find formerly available plants. The ecosystem had been seriously altered and the medicines were gone. These medicines were not ceremonial ineffective superstitious quackery; it is generally acknowledged that at first contact Native medicine was fully as developed as European medicine and contributed much to that profession. In a 1932 study, for example, 59 key US pharmaceuticals were attributed directly to Native medicine. (Vogel: *vi*) From antimalarials to cathartics, from muscle relaxants to emetics, from adsorbents to rubefacients, Native medicine was a robust and complex art, totally dependent upon an ecosystemic homeostasis that had essentially existed since the last Ice Age. This dynamically stable ecological balance was not a dioramic zone of lifeless eternal tableau, but it had robust enough internal regulatory processes to counteract disturbance to its overall health and utility.

The invasion of European militaries changed that. The subsequent occupation and enforced ecosystem destruction—in the practices of both depleting agriculture and extractive industry—finished the job. Native peoples have lost 3.53 million square miles just to the United States alone and none of it was freely given. The First Nations lost another 3.85 million square miles to Canada and some of that also remains under attack by the militaries.

When peace scholar Johan Galtung writes of the new point of view on so-called Third World nations as not under-developed or developing but rather as *mal*developed, we find the same phenomenon here in the US. Scholar Thomas Vennum, Jr. of the Smithsonian Institute documents the lifeways of the Ojibwe as they lived before contact with European invaders. The economy of the peoples in this western Great Lakes bioregion was a perfect example of the mutually exclusive nature of Native and European-style economies. Each band had an annual "route" through several distinct camps in their territory, each camp set up for the purpose of part-year living and resource gathering. Thus, a band might spend late winter and spring in a maple forest, gathering the sap to make syrup and sugar while also trapping and doing a little fishing. Then they would move to summer camp to do some planting, gathering, late summer harvesting and fishing. In the late summer or early fall they would head for wild rice camp and would also hunt and fish. (Vennum: 4) The ecology would recover between visits and the bounty was apparently endless. All that changed forever with the arrival of armed troops from Spain, Italy, then England and France.

Native peoples began the relationship as peacefully as they could, given the imperatives driving the Europeans, which were to obtain natural and human resources. This was of course the motive behind the Columbus voyage of 1492 and was the leitmotif of global expansion of European empires for the next 400 years. The formula was essentially the same for England, France, Spain, Holland, Portugal and Belgium: the great wars between the empires were funded by colonial extraction and the empire with the greatest reserves wins. This spelled disaster for native peoples everywhere and is a common story often told.

The motives were not entirely dissimilar as the US expanded and the reaction of the original inhabitants could hardly be surprising. In exasperation, they beseeched the US to act civilized, but to no avail. In a typical blandishment, Crow leader Bear Tooth told US commissioners gathered at Fort Laramie on 9 November 1867:

> *Fathers, fathers, fathers, hear me well. Call back your young men from the mountains of the bighorn sheep. They have run over our country; they have destroyed the growing wood and the green grass; they have set fire to our lands. Fathers, your young men have devastated the country and killed my animals, the elk, the deer, the antelope, my buffalo. They do not kill them to eat them; they leave them to rot where they fall. Fathers, if I went into your country to kill your animals, what would you say? Should I not be wrong, and would you not make war on me?*
>
> —Bear Tooth, 9 September 1867 (Brown: 144)

nuclear, biological, chemical war on Natives

A Shoshone woman dies of breast cancer, exposed to open-air nuclear testing in the 1950s. Her Native nation called the Shoshone land Newe Sogobia, encompassing most of the state of Nevada, and it was seized in direct contravention of the solemn Ruby Valley Treaty of 1863, only to be subjected to atomic attack beginning in 1951. (Harney: 209)

A Serpent River First Nation man finally speaks out against the lies and abuse of uranium mining corporations—Rio Algom and others—and the Canadian government. His reserve has hosted a dozen uranium mines, many of which were extracting the uranium for sale to the US nuclear weaponeers without bothering to tell the Native peoples what they were handling. Now more than 200 million tons of the radioactive tailings lurk behind seven massive earthen dams in the Serpent River watershed. (Rekmans: 15) The relatively young man has colon cancer, the scarce fish in the once-fecund river are suspect, and the corporations periodically make a token donation to a clean-up effort that has been largely a process of disturb and move, dig up and re-bury.

In the 19th century, the US military did damage to Native peoples and their lands by waging war directly on them. In the 20th century—and beyond—the US military and its attendant industries have done and continue to do damage to Native peoples and their lands by merely preparing to go to war against some other enemy.

This is clearly the case with regard to preparations to do atomic battle with the former Soviet Union; Natives and their lands were sacrificed, in the name of national security, to uranium mining. Native Americans, their lands and lifeways, were sacrificed to actual nuclear practice bombing. To complete the cycle of atomic attack, Natives were threatened with the permanent disposal of the radioactive trash left over from it all.

Radiological war on American indigenous peoples began with uranium, what some tribes called "angry rocks." Figures vary, but somewhere between 60 percent and 80 percent of all uranium reserves in the US lie on Native treaty land, 16 percent on the actual reservation land, and approximately one-fifth of all uranium mined in the US has been taken from beneath reservation land. (Grinde: 203) Of all proven recoverable reserves, half are in New Mexico and half of those lie beneath Navajo land. (Grinde: 206)

This nuclear arms connection began in the 1940s on Navajo land, where tribespeople started 30 years of going down in the mines for low pay and high risk. The raw material for the bombs that destroyed Hiroshima and Nagasaki came directly from Navajo land and the Navajos joined the Japanese as they paid the human health and ecological costs.

Following that relatively small start, production of uranium-based bombs and energy plants took off following the Atomic Energy Act of 1946, signed on 1 August by Harry Truman, creating the Atomic Energy Commission. The Navajo Nation and other tribes from the southwest didn't know it, but the government of the US had just declared war on tribal sovereignty in the name of national security. During much of World War II, the Manhattan Project secrecy covered the direct theft of uranium from mines on Navajo land, when no notice was given that uranium was being extracted from vanadium ore. It wasn't until 14 April 1944 that the mining corporation, VCA, even began to pay the Navajo for the uranium taken. (Eichstaedt: 33)

Ninety-nine percent of the uranium mined is waste and that effluent gives off ionizing radiation. Radioactive dust is carried off the open tailings piles by the winds to surrounding Native communities, though the Atomic Energy Commission told the tribes not to worry. (Grinde: 208)

Turns out—gosh, our mistake—that a 1978 Nuclear Waste Management Task Force report revealed that people living near the uranium tailings piles ran twice the risk of lung cancer as did the general population. (Grinde: 208) Scores of Navajos who lived near and/or worked in the mines died from lung cancer, according to the Coalition for Navajo Liberation. (Grinde: 208) There were no safety regulations when it began in the 1940s and there was no monitoring of Navajo miners' health then. The cancers began 20 to 30 years later and news broke just as another big uranium project was born on Native land to the north.

In January 1977 the US government announced the discovery of a rich uranium lode in the Precambrian rock formations at the eastern edge of *Paha Sapa*, the sacred Black Hills. Before April 15 there were more than 1,200 new claims and the rush was on. Given a moribund new nuclear power plant construction campaign, the uranium mines of the domestic US were no longer needed, but the damage goes on and on.

Uranium mining contaminates the Flathead Reservation in Montana, the Pine Ridge Reservation in South Dakota, The Wind River Reservation in Wyoming, and the Hopi and the Navajo Reservations in Arizona—and this does not include down-winder or down-water Native lands. (Harney: 220) Many Pueblo, Navajo, Hopi and other tribespeople have paid the ultimate price from working in those bomb mines.

> *We've created a monster, with no means of destroying it or neutralizing its effects, and we have no place to plant it. We cannot put it back into the Mother Earth as it is, since it's not the same as it was when it came out. It's been transformed into a monster.*
>
> —Bill Rosse, Sr., Western Shoshone (Harney: 131)

When military reservations lie near Native American reservations, are the environmental consequences somehow more acceptable? For many years in the late 1980s and early 1990s, the Pentagon seemed determined to locate military radioactive waste on Native land. "Bury my radioactive waste at Wounded Knee" might have been the lament. They have already achieved the same *de facto* result in several locales, including the Hanford Nuclear Reservation, where 36 million gallons of radioactive waste are stored in 177 underground tanks, at least 68 of which are leaking. Another 2,300 tons of spent nuclear fuel sits in leaky pools just a few hundred feet from the Columbia River. There are 25 tons of plutonium under armed guard. How can we overestimate the risk of dumping 440 *billion* gallons of radioactive liquid directly onto the ground in sight of the Columbia River during the site's 48-year active history (1943-1991)? Hanford Nuclear Reservation's 650 square miles are some of the most toxic on Earth. (Longley: 2, 5) This reservation borders the Yakima nation and is upstream from the Klickitats. Since its construction in 1943, prime contractor General Electric oversaw the release of approximately *twice* the radioactivity from Hanford as escaped from the April 1986 Chernobyl disaster. (Earth: 15)

"With over 900 bombs exploded, the Shoshone are the most bombed nation on Earth," asserted Chief Raymond Yowell of the Western Shoshone. (Harney: 131) When US open-air nuclear testing reached the point of the advent of giant thermonuclear hydrogen bombs, it was no longer possible to confine the effects to Western Shoshone and a few Mormons. The US singled out the island natives of the Bikini Atoll in the isolated and idyllic South Pacific, near the equator, for that series of tests, though the Truman administration began smaller tests some years earlier.

First, the American "liberators," welcomed by islanders who had been oppressed by Japanese invaders since the early part of the century, took their island and relocated the people to another, inferior island—Rongerik Atoll—which, at 125 miles distant from Ground Zero, was not nearly far enough away. Along with the navy's 5,400 rats, goats and pigs brought in for the purpose, the 167 Bikinians would be just more experimental subjects on which the Bomb would be used. They were miserable, starving and, after the hydrogen bomb testing begun on 1 March 1954, exposed to devastating levels of airborne radiation that caused cancers and birth defects. Their bodies, tested by the US government scientists, registered huge levels of cesium-137, plutonium 239 and 240. Regret was expressed. (Niedenthal: 1-10)

From the ELF antenna—the navy nuclear command facility located on Chequamegon National Forest land—which borders three Wisconsin Anishinabe reservations, to the Bravo 19 bombing range situated next to Walker River reservation—home to Paiute people—the military has been prepared to ignore ecological effects of their operations when they affect peoples of color. From unexploded ordnance to depleted uranium antitank shells, the ranges are toxic, exposing Native people to atmospheric and groundwater contamination. Low-level fighter and bomber jet practice runs are frequent jarring events on western US Native lands. Paiutes are kept busy with all this and the concern of military radioactive waste coming straight through the center of their Walker River reservation on its way to Yucca Mountain "disposal." They are also ten miles from a National Guard tank training area and near the Groom Mountains Area 51 top secret Stealth and Star Wars testing area. (McRoberts: 5) Should a nuclear bomb be accidentally dropped in the neighborhood, like the fictional *Broken Arrow* movie suggests, the Pentagon would have no obligation to reveal that information to the Paiutes or anyone else. And the Pentagon is even more secretive about its biological and chemical pollution of Native lands.

A tiny Goshute village is bordered by the Dugway Proving Ground, home of biological and chemical warfare testing for decades. On the small reservation itself is a rocket motor testing facility. (LaDuke: 105)

In Wisconsin, Ho-Chunk activists joined others in the Citizens for Safe Water Around Badger, stopped the army from continuing to pollute with the manufacture of ordnance and are now part of the reclamation effort. One of the dubious ecologically saving graces of this poor polluted place is that the ecology is grassland. The indigenous seed-eating birds are much less affected by toxic substances than are the omnivorous opportunists or the carnivorous birds. Thus, in the 1999 survey on land proximal to the former Badger Army Ammunition Plant, the Aldo Leopold Chapter of the Society for Conservation Biology found that the migratory birds in most trouble generally—grassland birds—are doing the best at Badger, probably because the grass wasn't plowed and dosed with pesticides. It was was left alone while local groundwater suffered the most instead. Indeed, the 15 species of the birds sighted on the former army land are either endangered or threatened in Wisconsin, a land where the grasslands long ago fell to the plow. Now the Ho-Chunk Nation is part of a peace conversion of the 7,500 acres of prairie flora and fauna that, in a toxicological sense, needs massive remediation, but in a ecological sense has retained a measure of the original potential for bison, elk and tallgrass; the land is forever worth fighting for. CSWAB, Ho-Chunk and others have been successful in stopping a transfer of that delicate prairie to the corporate-friendly state government, thus helping to preserve the chances for a true restoration effort. (Iltis: 7) On other Native lands, restoration will have to wait until they are no longer literally regarded as places for target practice.

Natives were generally relegated to the most inhospitable lands. Then, when certain subsurface resources were discovered, they were often removed from those lands formerly regarded as waste. Or, as was sometimes the case, they were literally targeted by the military while it was training to bomb the "real" enemy. Once again, one might wonder if one were a Native Shoshone, a Paiute, an islander from Hawaii or Vieques, who will save us from our "defenders"?

Kyle Kajihiro, a Hawaiian, wrote about this in a letter to the Honolulu Star-Bulletin on 2 March 2000. He described his visit to Vieques with an international peace delegation. Kajihiro compared the stunning beauty of the Puerto Rican island to that of Kahoolawe, one of the Hawaiian islands, and his similar feelings of witnessing colonialism and militarism upon observing the wasted land, the skeletons of tanks and planes, the lifelessness of the bombing range where the native ecology would have otherwise guaranteed an idyll teeming with tropical fecundity.

> *Unlike Kahoolawe, 9,400 residents live on Vieques and are affected by the bombing. Contaminants, including depleted uranium and heavy metals, migrate on the wind to populated areas, where they turn up in*

> *the drinking water or form thick clouds over the town. Many suspect that these contaminants cause the abnormally high cancer rate in Vieques, as much as 28 percent higher than in the rest of Puerto Rico. Militarization has crippled economic development on Vieques. With three-fourths of the island occupied by the navy, there is little land to farm. Bountiful ocean resources are off-limits to fishermen, and the visitor industry is stifled by military restriction and hazards.* (Kajihiro)

forced resource extraction from Native lands

> *It was in the summer of my twentieth year (1883) that I performed the ceremony of the elk. That fall, they say, the last of the bison herds was slaughtered by the Wasichus. I can remember when the bison were so many that they could not be counted, but more and more Wasichus came to kill them until there were only heaps of bones scattered where they used to be. The Wasichus did not kill them to eat; they killed them for the metal that makes them crazy, and they took only the hides to sell. Sometimes they did not even take the hides, only the tongues; and I have heard that fire-boats came down the Missouri River loaded with dried bison tongues. You can see that the men who did this were crazy.*
>
> —Black Elk, Oglala Holy Man (Neihardt: 213)

Throughout US history, the military has both extracted from, and been employed to defend the extraction of, resources from Native lands. These extractions result in decidedly negative outcomes for both the tribes and the land. Treaties have not stood in the way much and, in the 19th century, were not worth the paper they were printed on if valuable resources were located on "reserved" Native lands. The signal example of such was the Black Hills, where ("the metal that makes them crazy") was found and where Custer made war on Natives to allow whites in to extract that gold. His folly at the Little Bighorn on 25 June 1876 was a Native victory in battle but still a part of their overall strategic ecowar defeat.

The Black Hills resource extractive conflicts were updated in the 1970s, when uranium mining corporations moved in and Native peoples began to resist, attempting to invoke treaty law. "Uranium leases on treaty land in the Black Hills that were being issued quietly if not secretly to the huge energy consortiums might be delayed by prolonged treaty hearings in the courts." (Matthiessen: 56) The multinational, multipronged effort to circumvent the treaty law led to direct and violent conflict in the Black Hills in 1972, the result of which was an armed stand-off between the

American Indian Movement and the FBI, the murder of two FBI agents and several AIM members, the imprisonment of AIM members and the ongoing pollution of Native lands by the mining and processing of uranium.

Less toxically but just as egregiously, perhaps, the military was called in to protect Weyerhauser lumbermen from White Earth Anishinabeg in 1893. It took just a few years of 70 million board-feet cut to wipe out the huge white pine and sugar maple. (LaDuke: 118) This is the kind of cyclical theft and wastage that US armed forces have inflicted on Natives both here and abroad for more than 500 years.

Militaries grab the resources for their own use. But the military, as ever, grabs its share of whatever resources it needs when those resources are scarce and the "competition" is a tribal community.

When the US navy built its Fallon Naval Air Station in the Nevada desert, for example, they looked around for scarce water and moved in on the Truckee River, which empties into Pyramid Lake. This is a freshwater salmon system, a living and spawning riparian ecosystem for the cui-ui species and when the water levels grew alarmingly low the Pyramid Lake Paiute brought suit in federal court. They sought to enjoin the navy from further drain-downs and court ruled in favor of the navy, which is a general pattern when it comes to military environmental culpability. (Dycus: 32)

other militaries, other indigenous peoples

Of course, the Native peoples of North America are not the only indigenous peoples who suffer disproportionately from the activities of various militaries.

An Innu family in the quiet Nitassinan boreal forest is suddenly overwhelmed with physically painful and damaging decibels from a NATO training flight scarcely 75 meters above their heads. The father, mother and children scream as they cover their ears and fall to the forest floor. Nearby, a fox eats her kit in the forest.

And while the Shoshone nation was most bombed, the nations next in line for that sad honor are all nations—if not nation-states—that have never consented to being atom-bombed. In a terrible tragedy of mirror-image arms racism in the Soviet Union, they chose to blow off their dirty nukes in native lands in Kazakhstan. "I have traveled to Kazakhstan and witnessed some very sad things," wrote Corbin Harney in a letter to Bill Clinton in 1993. *"They cannot use their water any more due to contamination.... I have seen the effects of nuclear radiation, both in our country among the 'down-winders' and in Kazakhstan: children being born with eyes over their ears, arms coming out of their sides, and many other birth defects, as well as leukemia and cancers among the adults after only a short time."* (Harney: 166) Indeed, SU open-air testing and Chinese open-air testing alike seemed to be designed to attack their buffer populations, the indigenous, ethnically disfavored peoples that are more proximal to that other, enemy target nation. The Han Chinese bombed the indigenous Uygurs, the French bombed Tuamotu Island people and Great Britain bombed Australian Aboriginals. (Nietschman) To better threaten other nations, we atomic clubbers demonstrate the hideous effects on our own Native peoples, inflicting one last defeat on them. The Chinese bomb doesn't exist to protect their Tibetan citizens, the Soviet bomb was never meant to protect the Central Asians, the French bomb is meant to protect Paris, not Corsica, and the US bomb is meant to shield Washington, not Lakota or Pueblo lands.

In one of the most complex of all invader-indigenous relationships, the Israeli Defense Force commits environmental insult to the lands of the Palestinian indigenous peoples even as it withholds water from them and drives them from pillar to post in a shifting migratory flight that has now lasted more than half a century. The ongoing levels of fear are periodically reinforced; when Israel invaded Lebanon in 1982, some 20,000 were killed, 80 percent of whom were civilians. At the massacre of Sabra and Shatila alone, on September 12 of that year, the IDF tacitly arranged and supported the slaughter of 3,500 refugees in the pen of a camp by Christian militia fanatics. Refugees from the 1967 war total some 322,750. The Gulf War saw the expulsion of virtually all of the estimated 400,000 Palestinians from Kuwait to Jordan and the refugee camps from the 1948 war are still harboring the descendants of those driven from their homelands back then. (Ben Efrat: 141)

Some indigenous peoples are fighting back.

The Innu people of Nitassinan, including elders in their 80s, are engaged in nonviolent resistance to the NATO low level flights over their land in what Canada calls Labrador. Native women initiated the campaign—"mother-led band of peace warriors" was the *Toronto Now* description—and some have been acquitted, even when they have occupied the runway in the path of 500-ton war jets. (LaDuke: 57) The court ruled that the Innu could not be charged with trespassing on their own land. Regrettably, the Canadian Environmental Review Panel ruled in 1995 that the effects of the low-level flights were inconclusive and recommended doubling them. The fight for reclamation of Innu land and lifeways continues. (LaDuke: 58) The fight for a cessation of the desecration of Native lands in general is ongoing.

It is demonstrable that the militaries of the world care little for the Earth except as a source for matériel, as a staging ground for troops and as a launch platform for their war machines; their long record of environmental destruction during war and the preparation for war is undeniable.

Similarly, and related, the militaristic and imperialistic disregard for the lives, lands and lifeways of indigenous peoples have been documented by actions too numerous to count.

Nevertheless, there has been precious little coalition of the peace movement, Native Rights movement and environmental movement except nervously, locally and temporarily. Part of the problem is the lack of interdisciplinary study of the confluence of interest areas, which is where the interdiscipline of Peace Studies ought to be making a contribution. When we do, seriously and continuously, we may be part of a birthing of a new being, that Holy Grail we call coalition, that which Dr. King died for, that which Gandhi died for, that which has eluded us too long and which is the key to achieving a disarmed, just peace, a truly positive peace.

sources

Ben Efrat, Roni, "After Oslo: The Roots of the Israeli-Palestinian Conflict Still Unsolved," in Foerstel, Lenora, ***Creating Surplus Populations: The Effect of Military and Corporate Policies on Indigenous Peoples***. Washington DC: Maisonneuve Press, 1996: 141-146.

Brander, Robert, interview, spring 1989.

Brown, Dee, ***Bury My Heart at Wounded Knee: An Indian History of the American West***. NYC: Henry Holt & Company, 1970.

Burns, Robert, "White House panel says practice bombing on island should go on," *Duluth News-Tribune*, Associated Press, 19 October 1999: 3A.

Dycus, Stephen, ***National Defense and the Environment***. Hanover NH: University Press of New England, 1996.

Eichstaedt, Peter H., ***If You Poison Us: Uranium and Native Americans***. Santa Fe NM: Red Crane Books, 1994.

Grinde, Donald A. & Bruce E. Johansen, ***Ecocide of Native America***. Santa Fe NM: Clear Light Publishers, 1995.

Harney, Corbin, ***The Way It Is: One Water...One Air...One Mother Earth...***. Nevada City CA: Blue Dolphin Publishing, 1995.

Iltis, Hugh H. and Donald M Waller, "Badger Prairie: the last great chance," CSWAB newsletter, Winter 1999: 7.

INFACT, "Nuclear GEnocide," *Earth Island Journal*, Fall 1991: 15.

Kajihiro, Kyle, "Struggle in Vieques mirrors Kahoolawe," Honolulu Star-Bulletin, 2 March 2000.

LaDuke, Winona, ***All Our Relations: Native Struggles for Land and Life***. Cambridge MA: South End Press, 1999.

Libby, Ronald T., ***Eco-wars: Political Campaigns and Social Movements***. NYC: Columbia University Press, 1998.

Longley, Robert, "Hanford Site: Past Horror, Future Hope." http://usgovinfo.com/library/weekly/aa102497.htm , 8 March 1999.

Mander, Jerry, ***In the Absence of the Sacred: The Failure of Technology and the Survival of the Indian Nations***. San Francisco: Sierra Club Books, 1991.

Matthiessen, Peter, ***In the Spirit of Crazy Horse***. NYC: Viking, 1991, original

1980.

McRoberts, LeAnn, "Paiutes vs. Pentagon," *Red Nations Movement*, October 1991: 5-9.

Morgan, Larry Cloud, ***Prison Meditations***, Minneapolis: St. Joseph's House, 1985.

Niedenthal, Jack, "A Short History of the People of the Bikini Atoll," http://www.bikiniatoll.com/history.html, 22 March 1999.

Neihardt, John G., ***Black Elk Speaks: Being the Life Story or a Holy Man of the Oglala Sioux***, Lincoln NE: University of Nebraska Press, 1988, original 1932.

Nietschman, Bernard & William Le Bon, "Nuclear Weapon States and Fourth World Nations," *Western Shoshone Defense Project Newsletter*, Winter/Spring 1995.

Rekmans, Lorraine, Keith Lewis and Anabel Dwyer, ***This Is My Homeland: Stories of the Effects of Nuclear Industries by People of the Serpent River First Nation and the North Shore of Lake Huron.*** Cutler, Ontario, Canada: Serpent River First Nation, 1999.

Vennum, Thomas, Jr., ***Wild Rice and the Ojibwe People***, Washington DC: Smithsonian Institute, 1986.

Vogel, Virgil J., ***American Indian Medicine***. Norman OK: University of Oklahoma Press, 1970.

Section 2: Shooting Wars: Mother Earth as collateral damage

> *In chthonic perspective sin tends to be conceived as pollution, vividly symbolized in the spilling of a murdered man's blood upon the land. Such sin carries its own penalty: community life is tainted and sickened, producing blight and pestilence. Release from the evil must be sought in a symbolic act of cleansing which is outwardly ritualistic and inwardly redemptive.* (Wheelwright: 283)

> *With a note of joy in his voice, an old farmer told us, "I've been living in this area for over fifty years, since before 1940. And I've seen the bombings, toxic chemicals, and napalm drive the sarus cranes away from the Plain of Reeds. We had thought we would never again see those graceful birds. But now they have returned...It's a great joy for us. They bring happiness to our plain."* (Quy: 40)

When the toxic preparation for war turns to actual firing of weapons toward the enemy, the Earth begins to suffer much more widespread, immediate damage—and that environmental destruction is ironically more easily ignored. Certainly a soldier's first thought during real-bullet fighting is not going to be the protection of the arable soil or potable water; he is looking to survive. A nation's citizenry is aroused to spill blood, not to avoid spilling jet fuel. The media will cover the crippling effect of bomb strikes on the enemy, not the future crippling mutagenic effects of toxic contamination of a missile strike on a chemical plant on the fetus of a local mother or wife of a returning soldier.

Consider this contradiction. When the mere build-up toward the 1991 Gulf War began as Desert Shield in the late summer and through the fall of 1990, then-president Bush went to Congress to insist on a suspension of all environmental laws as they might apply to the military, in order to meet this national crisis. Congress caved virtually without a murmur.

Then, when Saddam Hussein threatened to fire the Kuwait oil wellheads if the US attacked, Senator Joseph Lieberman (D-Conn) demanded that Hussein be put to death as an environmental criminal.

Can we say "double standard"?

The truth is that the Earth is simply regarded as a tool to be used for one army's advantage over another. If that means salting the fields with 110 million landmines in 63 nations around the Earth (Hallock: 160), then that is what is necessary. If bombing leaves toxic craters across the countryside, that is part of war. If fuel depots are targeted, as they were by NATO during the 1999 air attack on Serbia, then the resultant air and water pollution is merely a side effect of the mission—which is to deprive the enemy of fuel for troop movement. If troops carry disease and introduce a plague in a native population—e.g. the infection of Mexican natives with unheard of measles and smallpox by invading Spanish troops in the early 16th century (Schwartz: 34)—that's just Mother Nature's long-distance weapon. The last thing any of the conflictual parties considered in Poland between September 1939 and May 1945—the five-year, eight-month period of war in that poor country during a World War that began on Polish soil—was the environment. By the conclusion of that worldwide conflict, Poland emerged with the dubious distinction of suffering the highest mortality rate—some 17 percent of its population, and with a saturation of unexploded ordnance in its lands and adjacent seas. Bombs, artillery and mortar shells, anti-tank mines, anti-personnel mines, grenades and anti-ship mines remained, courtesy of German, Polish, Soviet, US and British forces. Apart from the somewhat mapped minefields—covering some 25 million hectares, or 80 percent of the entire country—the unexploded ordnance was impossible to map. The Polish Ministry of Defense continues to "neutralize" this eco-disaster; between 1945-1956 they exploded or otherwise destroyed some 73 million separate pieces of remnant explosives and nearly another 15 million between 1956 and 1982. "Some 460 disposal personnel have been killed in the line of duty in Poland during the four decades following World War II," with hundreds more wounded. (Molski: 27) Thousands of civilians—children, women and men—have been sacrificed despite these literally heroic clean-up efforts.

There is no compendious source of all ecological damage caused by war through the ages; society hasn't valued that particular aspect of war enough to bother to keep track of such things. What we can promote is a perspective leading society to think about the costs of war as that society considers not only a particular war but war in general. When we talk and write about World War I, then, we ought to note that farmers in France continue to be blown apart by mines laid there so long ago. For that matter, when we talk about the Prussian wars of the 1870s, we ought to mention that live white phosphorus mines from that early era are still occasionally unearthed, sometimes to lethal effect. Post-conflict casualties never get in the history books as attributed to war, thus giving a false sense of closure on the cost side of the analysis.

When we discuss World War II, we don't often consider the massive outbreak of tularemia amongst German panzer troops in Southern Russia, followed immediately by an even worse such outbreak amongst Russian troops and civilians. The incidence convinced bioweaponeer Ken Alibek that his nation, the Soviet Union, had used some kind of aerosol delivery of tularemia against the Germans, which was made immeasurably worse either by a sudden shift in wind or by contaminated rodents carrying the disease to the local Russian communities. Approximately 100,000 cases caused an order-of-magnitude spike in the epidemiological norm of 10,000 cases annually in Russia. (Alibek: 30) Whether intentionally or not, war breeds disease and ecological failure.

We *do* think of the obvious and spooky ecological damage when we ponder the two atomic bombs dropped during a war on Hiroshima and Nagasaki. The eerie notion that a grandson of a *hibakusha* (survivor of one of those bombings) may develop improperly as a result of inherited harm is devilish, Satanic, accursed. We are, presumably, chastised by the enormity of nuclear poisoning. "Why preparations are still going on for more nuclear weapons is beyond the rational logic of any man or woman," wrote Nobel Peace Laureate Alva Myrdal. (Peterson: *vii*) She wrote that in an introduction to a book, ***Aftermath***, which first details the local ecological devastation of Hiroshima and Nagasaki and then posits that on a global scale if nuclear weaponry is used nowadays. But she wrote her lament almost two decades ago, in May 1983. It seems that the human health implications of the war potential locked in the nuclear arsenals of the world have still not convinced humanity to disarm these unusable tools of unthinkable nuclear holocaust.

"A single American B-52 strategic nuclear bomber can now carry more explosive power than that used in all the wars in history." (Barnaby: 2) The same is true, still, for the Trident submarines, since they carry more nuclear firepower than do the B-52 or B-1 bombers. The scientific community concluded time and again that the results of nuclear war would be devastating not just for the target nation, not just the region, but for entire hemispheres, even the entire planet, and possibly even for the very future of life on Earth. Nuclear war would immediately deliver radiation sickness to those experiencing the fallout and would mean an epidemiological nightmare of disease. Nuclear autumn or nuclear winter would make food crop production impossible for seasons, years, maybe decades, assuring starvation to survivors everywhere. Freshwater would be contaminated terribly on a spreading and deepening basis and the oceans would undergo severe ecological strain, perhaps mass die-off. In short, the medical, food, water, energy, economic and human health consequences of any nuclear war would be the worst disaster ever to strike humanity. As with so many of the modern effects of war in an era of high tech weaponry, the members of the military would be affected *less* than would civilians, adults *less* than children, the strong *less* than the weak. One hundred rads per day of radiation for one week, not much to expect in a nuclear war, may not penetrate to the bone marrow of an adult but would be much more likely to do so in a smaller-bodied child. Bone marrow is particularly vulnerable to radiation, especially in a timeframe of weeks, months or years. When the military says a casualty is likely from a weapon, they mean immediately and they speak in thousands of rads, but that is not by any means the sum of the problem. (Lindop: 91) A single 1MT thermonuclear burst over an urban area of four million would likely result in approximately 800,000 fatalities and 1.7 million casualties. (Kendall: 79) This kind of math is stark, in raw contrast to the words "defense" or "protect" or "legitimate use."

And even with the gift of time, the grace period following the end of the Cold War, humanity has not succeeded in ridding itself of this scourge. Jonathan Schell, whose 1982 ***Fate of the Earth*** so sharply touched humankind when he wrote about the potential for our species' thermonuclear demise, has challenged humanity to awaken to the window of opportunity. We have to wonder, along with Alva Myrdal, if we will see the Hiroshima past and accept it as our collective future or if we will grow a communal backbone and take these diabolical machines apart, for good…and then begin dismantling the entire bloody war system, for good.

sources

Alibek, Ken, ***Biohazard: The Chilling True Story of the Largest Covert Biological Weapons Program in the World—Told from the Inside by the Man Who Ran It***. NYC: Random House, 1999.

Barnaby, Frank, "The Effects of Nuclear Weapons," in ***The Aftermath: The Human and Ecological Consequences of Nuclear War***. Jeannie Peterson, editor. NYC: Pantheon Books, 1983.

Hallock, Daniel, ***Hell, Healing and Resistance: Veterans Speak***. Farmington PA: The Plough Publishing House, 1998.

Kendall, Henry, "The effects of a nuclear war in Europe," in Tromp, H.W. & G.R. LaRocque, editors, ***Nuclear War in Europe***. Groningen, Denmark: Groningen University Press, 1981 (77-86).

Lindop, Patricia, "Radiation aspects of a nuclear war in Europe," in Tromp, H.W. & G.R. LaRocque, editors, ***Nuclear War in Europe***. Groningen, Denmark: Groningen University Press, 1981 (87-113).

Molski, Boguslaw A. and Jan Pajak, "Explosive remnants of World War II in Poland," in Westing, Arthur H., editor, ***Explosive Remnants of War: Mitigating the Environmental Effects***. London: Taylor & Francis, 1985 (17-

32)

Peterson, Jeannie, editor, ***The Aftermath: The Human and Ecological Consequences of Nuclear War***. NYC: Pantheon Books, 1983.

Quy, Vo, "On the Wings of Peace," in *Natural History*, November 1990: 40-41.

Schwartz, Stuart B., ***Victors and Vanquished: Spanish and Nahua Views of the Conquest of Mexico***. Boston: Bedford/St. Martin's, 2000.

Tromp, H.W. & G.R. LaRocque, editors, ***Nuclear War in Europe***. Groningen, Denmark: Groningen University Press, 1981.

Westing, Arthur H., editor, ***Explosive Remnants of War: Mitigating the Environmental Effects***. London: Taylor & Francis, 1985.

Wheelwright, Philip, editor, ***The Presocratics***. NYC: Macmillan Publishing Company, 1966.

From Carthage to Vietnam: salting, spraying, cratering

Some religious folks around the CW were loath to distribute the paper after Pearl Harbor. I goodnaturedly kidded them by calling their liturgy an excuse for lethargy.

—Ammon Hennacy (Hennacy: 58)

The girl in one of the Vietnamese Peace Villages is 15. Her skin below her neck is black...her back is covered with sagging tumors. Her father was sprayed with Agent Orange. Her friends back home call her "Water Buffalo." She is sad because they think she looks like a water buffalo.

—Dan Zwerdling, NPR/American Radio Works report, ***Vietnam: A Nation, Not a War,*** April 2000 (Zwerdling)

There is always ecological damage from war, even if limited to a transmogrification of green fields to mud fields. Armies, says the Tao te Ching, are always followed by thornbushes, which is to say, the pioneer plants that recolonize trampled Earth are often those barbed plants which specialize in active, sharp personal and collective defense. People are no different; when attacked, our fresh, tender and humorous compassion is trampled and our prickly side emerges. Catholic Worker activist Ammon Hennacy fought this with his whole being. Following Japan's awful attack on Pearl Harbor he rose to meet the thorny reaction with humor and fearlessness, knowing the wisdom of the ancients, anticipating the wisdom of psychologist Eric Berne. Berne would note our behavioral cycles in the early 1960s and he would finally assert that they are so powerful that the only way to stop it is to stop it; we must decide to evolve past this business of war on each other and the Earth. We simply must stop it.

We count our war dead and regard that as the primary cost of war, which it is. We note the destruction of bridges and buildings and count that as a cost of war, which it surely is. But we don't figure in the environmental pricetag of violent social conflict, though it has been with us at the very least since Abimelech's troops spread salt on the conquered city of Shechem (Judgments 9:45). The Nablus, Jordan region (where Shechem was) was then the possible birthplace of chemical warfare with its toxic ecological damage. (Nietschmann: 35)

When the Spanish invaded Mexico, they unwittingly carried with them the infectious diseases that had already decimated Europe, diseases for which the Native American peoples had no natural defense. The resultant plague won the war for the invaders over the *Mexica* troops under the last emperor, Cuahtemoc, with the final conquest of Tenochtitlan by gun, sword and plague. Indeed, smallpox elevated Cuahtemoc himself to the position of the last *tlatoani* when Cuitlahoc succumbed to the disease. (Schwartz: 182) The arrival of disease-ridden Old Worlders has wreaked havoc on the human health of Native Americans north and south since the original Colombian contact in 1492. Entire villages deep inland, from the Mississippi River south through the Americas, were drastically affected long before first arrival in their villages of invading Europeans. Traveling Natives spread the disease from the coasts inward faster than the Euro armies could gain ground—the original over-the-horizon attack. By the time those invaders came to some areas, those places were undefended and untended by the sick and dead remains of a once-vibrant people. That's just war, we say. The effects have a long and twisted reach. And even though the Spaniards would have spread the diseases even if they arrived in peace, the reality is that the mobile populations that spread disease are more often than not either warriors or war refugees. Either way, war has decimated by disease throughout history.

A drylands grain farmer in Libya, born in 1979, turns the soil one season and is killed by an explosion. He is a casualty, in the year 2000, of World War II, putatively concluded in August, 1945, a war which most would consider in terms of Europe and the Pacific.

Thousands of Libyans have been killed from the ordnance strewn about, mostly by British and German forces, even though the land was a colony of Italy then. Some five million mines, both anti-personnel and anti-tank, were deployed and they still kill Libyans today, especially in the desperately needed grain farmlands upon which the country depends. (Sgaier: 33) This environmental impact of war—this salting of the fields—haunts us long after the landmine ban has legally taken effect; the dead farmer is not concerned with this new law.

US vs Vietnam, people and land

Sometimes, as we learned in the war in Indochina, a grenade is more than just a grenade; it is a landmine. In a war against illiterate and nearly Stone Age peasants, the mighty US expended some 140 million M-406 grenades, which are now reckoned as "the single most culpable explosive remnant in producing post-war casualties." (Martin: 43) The US went to war in Vietnam by slippery increments and, by the time it was over, had ruined much of the land through the use of landmines and chemical warfare. As with many wars in history, ruining the environment was no mere collateral damage, no accident at all; it was an objective, part of the point, to deprive "him" of food, refuge, cover and a staging ground for attack. (Nietschmann: 35) More than 11.2 million gallons of Agent Orange and seven million gallons of other poisonous defoliants—Agents Blue and White, named for the colors on the 55-gallon drums in which they were shipped—were sprayed on the mangrove swamps and jungles of that poor, small nation in order to bring it to its knees. (Hallock: 144) "It is estimated that one million Vietnamese were poisoned between 1966 and 1969." (Bertell: 148) In addition to chemical warfare, more ordnance were fired on that little nation by the US in that war than it used in all theaters for the entire World War II, at least 14.3 million tons of air, ground and sea munitions. (Martin: 39) Craters still visible from the air pock one-third of the nation. Like smallpox writ large on the face of Mother Earth, these craters recount the days of disfigurement essentially forever.

When war begins, the rivers are soon filled with the rubble from bridges, the hazardous chemicals from bombed fuel depots and chemical plants, and the untreated sewage from cities with destroyed infrastructures. Traveling the Ohio River valley in the US or the Rohr in Germany, it is obvious that the chemical and electrical generation plants are clustered along these waterways for purposes of transport, cooling and dilution of pollution. This, to some greater or lesser extent, is how it is for many of the world's riparian environments; they are valuable and vulnerable. Even in "primitive" regions, war shoots the riverine ecology full of big holes. Certainly the Mekong was one.

As I picked him off the couch that the Veterans Hospital ambulance attendants had dumped him on to die, I looked at him. As I joined my sister and nieces in laying him on his hospice deathbed in the "living room" of their small home, I peered into the gaunt face and hollow eyes of a working class American man, taken as a kid to go to those jungles of Vietnam. That is where those boys were frequently exposed to various chemical warfare agents. "It sat in the mess halls, in barrels along the wall," he told his wife, Leesa, years later. Those were 55-gallon barrels with colored stripes, including the orange stripes most often, called Agent Orange. (Gilmore) Tim Gilmore was declared an official victim of Agent Orange and, along with a few thousand others, was grudgingly granted a small compensatory amount for his sacrifice after battling the Pentagon and Dow Chemical in court for the token award. Indeed, it took an intervention from US Senator Paul Wellstone (D-Minn.) to expedite Tim's case toward resolution before he died. On a warm, sunny June day, with blooming flowers and twittering birds just outside the window, with Tim lying helpless in bed just two feet away, I read his medical file at the Veterans Hospital in Minneapolis, Minnesota. The report actually began with the words, "This poor man..." and went on to describe a series of more than 40 inoperable tumors running from his brain down his spine and on into his lungs. Back in their small home later that day, I listened to his death rattle and fed him liquid morphine. He finally died two days later, after his wife and daughters told him, on Fathers Day, 1995, "You can go now. It's OK. We'll be OK." He had outlived his prognosis by more than a year, suffering tremendous pain but living to see his oldest daughter graduate from high school three days before. We wheeled him in there, a wisp of a man, former weight lifter, former runner, former tough guy from a military family, reduced to gray skin, tumorous bones and longing eyes. Since Tim was part Native American, I burned fragrant, ceremonial sweetgrass as I delivered his eulogy in the Fort Snelling chapel. Vietnamese farmer and former fighter Nguyen Hu Thanh, who suffers from a painful central nervous system disease and whose 22-year-old son was born with Down's Syndrome, said the Agent Orange "smelled like a perfume." (Dreyfuss: 46)

That is the legacy of war in Vietnam. How many more walls would we need in Washington DC to include the names of the suicides and Agent Orange victims who have died since the end of the war, since the gunfire stopped and the poison of body and mind set to work? Some say the 58,000 carved names represent about one-quarter of the American mortalities. How many more walls would we need to include the Vietnamese victims? They were as many as three million by some estimates, just from the combat period, not to mention the post-peace-agreement birth defects and cancers amongst those poor people. The US hit almost a third of their entire country with various bombs, shells or defoliants, leaving some 250 million pockmarks on the Earth in that small nation and destroying some eight percent of the crops, 14 percent of the jungle and half the mangroves (Nietschmann: 35); there were scant hiding places for the Vietnamese people and there was nowhere to hide from the "sophisticated" health effects. They have no fancy VA hospitals, they have no court cases to award the survivors any compensation. They are simple and tragic victims of the way war is waged in the technologically advanced times in which we live and die.

As grudgingly as the Pentagon has been to give aid and comfort to the raw recruits that it so liberally sacrificed from this country, we are not surprised that the US government—driven from a "backward" jungle country by a populace in raggedy black "pajamas,"—has completely denied any aid to the "victors," the Vietnamese victims of its chemical warfare. (Myre: 5A) At the same time, the US state department tells the Vietnamese government that in order to establish the trust that might lead to sharing medical findings on treating the effects of this chemical warfare, the government of that impoverished rainforest mountain nation must account for US MIA troops.

Trust. The American boys trusted their government; it was worth fighting for, wasn't it? The Vietnamese opponents—the enemies of colonial invaders of their homeland—those soldiers and those people were utterly unaware of what chemical warfare really meant. All they knew was, when the planes passed over in broad formation and sprayed the ubiquitous mist, the foliage died within a day or two, and they would have to move their field hospitals and base camps yet again. They had no idea that the spray included dioxin, the most potent anti-life chemical ever concocted by scientists. When the fish died in the jungle waters, "What did we know?" asked Le Cao Dai, a Hanoi surgeon and veteran of the long campaigns to evict all foreign military invaders from the French onward. "The soldiers simply caught the fish and ate them." (Dreyfuss: 44) And they didn't protect themselves from the spray—their concern was getting shot, blown apart or engulfed in flames. They had no clue about chemical warfare, especially slow-acting (on humans) deadly chemicals.

In retrospect, what the US did with Agent Orange was simply a sophisticated version of what the Sioux used to do when battling an enemy; the warriors from the plains burnt the prairie in fire-drives to deprive the enemy of game and cover. Scorched-earth policy is nothing new, and was also used by the North against the Confederacy in the US Civil War, by the UK against the Mau Mau in Kenya (1950-1956), by France against the long-and-still-suffering Algerians (1949-1962) by the FSU against the Afghani mujaheddin (1979-1989), and most recently in southern Sudan, Eritrea, Tigray, Chittagong Hill Tracts, Kawthoolei, East Timor, El Salvador and Guatemala (Nietschmann: 35) But the ecological effects of the hunter-gatherer acts of eco-warfare lasted a short time before complete recovery of the Earth. In Vietnam, the defoliation and fish death were only the beginning.

Soil tests done in various representative regions of Vietnam more than a decade after herbicide spraying revealed three major effects and numerous smaller consequences. Soil erosion has been massive. Soil creep on steep hills and mountains has been significant. And mobile iron—i.e. the essential soil element assimilable by plants and then by the consumers—has been drastically reduced. (Huây: 69)

In one post-war forestry study of 168,430 hectares of inland evergreen forest in the Ma Da reserve, it was learned that the "rich" diversity was reduced 100 percent to zero, that the treeless area increased by 164 percent and that those changes were virtually entirely due to war damage. Worse, presumably due to chemical damage and soil perturbation (exposure of sterile subsoil), there was, by 1981-1982 studies, "almost no natural regeneration of forest trees in the zone of destruction." (Hiêp: 31) This remains the condition in 2000, due in large part to lack of resources required for replanting. (Zwerdling)

Then the humans began to suffer. By the early 1970s, the incidence of certain health problems all elevated: cancers, immune-deficiency diseases, severe diarrhea, persistent malaria resistant to drug treatment, miscarriages, premature births, birth defects—including gross malformations. Estimates place Agent Orange-related birth defects alone at approximately half a million. As noted, neither the American government nor the chemical weapons manufacturer, Dow Chemical, has paid a dime toward any of these victims. (Dreyfuss: 44) The poisons were called herbicides; they were actually biocides, toxic to life. It was in response to what ecologists found in Vietnam that a new word was coined, in fact, ecocide, the kill-off of an entire eco-system. When, for example, the US murdered 54 percent of the mangrove coastal and river delta wetlands in the entire country of Vietnam, they virtually annihilated entire ecosystems that had been developing for thousands of years. Some say the 10-year total herbicide spray program, begun in 1961, amounted to more than 20 million gallons of chemicals. Add to this the eight most intense years of "conventional" bombing, mostly from B-52 Stratofortresses, raining destruction from some 2.8 million tons of bombs beginning in 1965. (Pfeiffer: 37) This level of focused environmental annihilation changes the recovery timeline, if indeed a restoration is even possible after such a war.

The impacts upon the Earth of waging war are, in virtually every instance, tremendous, from the creation of massive mudfields where ripe grain once waved to the brightly colored sheen of petrochemical waste in the puddles, in the spring (erstwhile) freshets, in the rushing mountain streams now choked with debris, on the surface of lakes now undrinkable and unfishable. From the first aerial bombardment by German zeppelins on 6 August 1914 on Liege, Belgium, during which 13 bombs were dropped and nine people were killed, to the mass air attack on Serbia and

Kosovo in the spring of 1999, the effects have been devastating. Just since the end of World War II, the US *alone* has bombed China (1945-46), Korea (1950-53), China again (1950-53), Guatemala (1954), Indonesia (1958), Cuba (1959-60), Guatemala again (1960), Congo (1964), Peru (1965), Laos (1964-73), Vietnam (1961-73), Cambodia (1969-70), Guatemala yet again (1967-69), Grenada (1983), Libya (1986), El Salvador (much of 1980s), Nicaragua (1980s), Panama (1989), Iraq (1991-9), Sudan (1998), Afghanistan (1998) and Yugoslavia (1999). (Jipson) Some bombardments were one raid, most were protracted proxy wars or direct US attacks; all were catastrophic for humans and the general ecology of the areas affected. In Vietnam, the millions of bomb craters have produced so much standing, fetid water that the post-war epidemics of mosquito-bred disease are simply called "bomb crater malaria." (Nietschmann: 35) The sheer magnitude of the lasting effects of all war, especially in our "advanced" era, is impossible to determine yet is crucial to acknowledge.

sources

Bertell, Rosalie, "The Re-greening of the Planet," in: Shiva, Vandana, ***Close to Home: Women Reconnect Ecology, Health and Development Worldwide***. Philadelphia: New Society Publishers, 1994.

Cvijovic, Drasko, e-mail, 1 November 1999.

Dreyfuss, Robert. "Apocalypse Still," *Mother Jones*, January/February 2000: 42-51+.

Fleishman, Jeffery, "Yugoslavia is afloat in 'war waste,'" *The Philadelphia Inquirer*, 14 October 1999.

Gilmore, Leesa, conversation, June 1995.

Hallock, Daniel, ***Hell, Healing and Resistance: Veterans Speak***. Farmington PA: The Plough Publishing House, 1998.

Hennacy, Ammon, ***The Book of Ammon***. 2nd edition. Baltimore: Fortkamp Publishing Company, 1994 (1st edition, 1965).

Hiêp, Dinh, "Long-term changes in dense inland forest following herbicidal attack," in Westing, Arthur H., editor, ***Herbicides in War: The Long-term Ecological and Human Consequences***. London: Taylor & Francis, 1984 (31-32)

Huây, Hoàng Van and Nguyên Xuan Cu, "Long-term changes in soil chemistry following herbicidal attack," in Westing, Arthur H., editor, ***Herbicides in War: The Long-term Ecological and Human Consequences***. London: Taylor & Francis, 1984 (69-73).

Jipson, Art, email, 30 April 1999, jipsonaj@muohio.edu

Martin, Earl S. and Murray Hiebert, "Explosive remnants of the Second Indochina War in Viet Nam and Laos," in Westing, Arthur H., editor, ***Explosive Remnants of War: Mitigating the Environmental Effects***. London: Taylor & Francis, 1985 (39-49).

Myre, Greg, "A Vietnamese general reminisces," AP, in *Duluth News-Tribune*, 9 April 2000: 5A.

Nietschmann, Bernard, "Battlefields of Ashes and Mud," in *Natural History*, November 1990: 35-37.

Pfeiffer, E.W., "Degreening Vietnam," in *Natural History*, November 1990: 37-40.

Quy, Vo, "On the Wings of Peace," in *Natural History*, November 1990: 40-41.

Schwartz, Stuart B., ***Victors and Vanquished: Spanish and Nahua Views of the Conquest of Mexico***. Boston: Bedford/St. Martin's, 2000.

Sgaier, Khairi, "Explosive remnants of World War II in Libya: impact on agricultural development," in Westing, Arthur H., editor, ***Explosive Remnants of War: Mitigating the Environmental Effects***. London: Taylor & Francis, 1985 (33-37).

Thomas, William, ***Scorched Earth: The Military's Assault on the Environment***. Gabriola Island, Vancouver, British Columbia: New Society Press, 1995.

Torch, Erik, eyewitness account, presented in Duluth MN, 8 November 1999.

Westing, Arthur H., editor, ***Herbicides in War: The Long-term Ecological and Human Consequences***. London: Taylor & Francis, 1984

Westing, Arthur H., editor, ***Explosive Remnants of War: Mitigating the Environmental Effects***. London: Taylor & Francis, 1985.

Zwerdling, Dan, NPR/American Radio Works report, ***Vietnam: A Nation, Not a War***, 29 April 2000.

UN vs Iraq, NATO vs Serbia: US leads attack on Earth

A gulf profound as that Serbonian Bog
Betwixt Damatia and mount Casius old,
Where Armies whole have sunk: the parching Air
Burns frore, and cold performs th' effect of Fire.
—John Milton, ***Paradise Lost***

Weapons of mass destruction are ***always*** *in the wrong hands.*
—Deepak Chopra, March 2000 (on India's nuclear weapons)

The US led both of the significant air wars of the 1990s: the 1991 Gulf War and the 1999 Kosovo/Serbia attack. The US rounded up support in the UN for the Gulf War but was rankled by dissent from two quarters. First, there were all the nations not naturally sympathetic to the rich, white, US attacking a relatively poor brown-skinned people. Second, there were all the NGOs housed in the UN, virtually all of them with missions antithetical to waging such warfare.

In the most recent largish war, the US-led NATO air forces hammered Yugoslavia and Kosovo. It was simpler and quicker, politically, for the US to convince that organization to use mass violence. It was also much easier for the rest of the world to grasp, politically, since NATO is not a peace-building organization in any sense, as the UN claims to be. NATO is quite baldly a military alliance of former colonial power northern nations, easily forced about by a bloated US military assuming a connatural role as global enforcer. The most telling moment that illuminated the difference between the two war coalitions might have been when, in late March 1999, a reporter asked US Secretary of State Madeleine Albright about China's and Russia's strong objections to the planned war on Yugoslavia. She responded laconically, as though that ended the matter, "Russia and China are not part of NATO." (National)

While Slobodan Milošević made no threats against the Earth analogous to those made by Saddam Hussein eight years previous, the US-led forces themselves did grave damage to the environment in both wars, setting post-Cold War precedent. Both wars were an ill augury for peace and for the Earth, though, in a kind of diplomatic diplophonia (the vocal ability to produce two separate notes simultaneously), both wars claimed to be in the interest of protecting—yes—peace and the environment. Oh—and the bombing, strafing, rocket fire, cruise missile attacks on electric power plants, HARM missile destruction of auto factories and the occasional stray rocket into neighboring Bulgaria were, as usual, "humanitarian."

Desert Storm of bombs, tanks, pollution

On January 25, 1991, ten days after the bombs began to fall in Kuwait and Iraq, the first of the oil spills gushed into the northern Persian Gulf, to be followed by some 11 million more barrels. Turns out that at least a third of that volume was released straight into the environment—mostly into the water—by allied bombs hitting Iraqi tankers and other obviously poor targets. (Pope: 36)

The outcome of the Gulf War was what we might have expected; Saddam said he'd fire his oil wells if he were attacked. He was and he did. George Bush put the Vietnam Syndrome—fear of a quagmire war of attrition—to rest. He did so by ordering a sudden and massive burst of violence after a long build-up of troops, of launching platforms and of tensions. Where the Iraqi military launched a total of 11 tons of SCUD missile weapons against Israel and Saudi Arabia, the US-led UN forces dropped 141,921 tons of bombs on Iraq and Kuwait. Compare that to the 3,421 tons dropped by the Allies on the massive attack on Dresden that resulted in a firestorm in February 1945. Gulf War US-led allies used approximately eight million gallons of oil during the "100-hour-ground-war," thus adding about 80,000 tons of carbon dioxide to the Greenhouse Effect. Meanwhile, Saddam's forces were adding another 100,000 tons per day from burning oil well heads. (Earth)

Prepping the Mideast for the Persian Gulf War began, in some ways, with the long war between Iraq and Iran during the 1980s, from which Iraq emerged as the OPEC policeman. Indeed, when 1990 oil prices tumbled from $18 per barrel to $14, many OPEC nations were grateful for Iraq's threat against Kuwait to stop overproduction. (Congressional: 180) The Gulf War began with a sudden air attack on 15 January 15 1991, and by February of that year the habitat for at least a quarter million wading birds on the Saudi Arabian coast was uninhabitable. (Thomas, 1995: 117) At a minimum, tens of thousands of cormorants and other water birds were killed outright by the more than 500 oil well fires and huge slicks. One of them, the largest oil slick in history, was a 600-square mile event that covered some 300 miles of coastline and presented a lethal zone to birds. The black precipitation from the fires fell as rain in the Mideast and as black snow as far as Kashmir, some 1,500 miles eastward. (Canby: 6) This is precisely the effect on the environment that we ought to be able to predict given intelligence on the weaponry and policies involved, yet it is not part of the calculations undertaken by the leaders of nation-states. While Saddam blames DU and many blame Saddam's oil fires, the fact is that the citizens of Iraq are experiencing a cancer epidemic due to the war. The war was waged by both sides without consideration for the Earth. Now, exacerbating and extending that war against life, the victims are dying faster due to the siege-like sanctions, which deny medicine and sanitation materials. War is the enemy and people are the victims, with the environment taking the hit in between.

Why is this? Part of this disconnect is racism, part militarism. Western well-rooted disdain for peoples of color, and our willingness to inflict horrific environmental and human health damage upon them during conflict is nowhere more baldly stated than Winston Churchill's 1919 memo about using chemical weapons on desert peoples: *"I am strongly in favor of using poisons gas against uncivilized tribes* [where it could] *spread a lively terror."* (Thomas, 1998: 9) Further, if we look at war historically, we find innumerable examples of environmental degradation and virtually no discussion beforehand of those potential effects. Of course, there is little public discussion beforehand about collateral damage—that is, the civilians and their civil society infrastructure—so why would we expect the decision-makers to take ecology into account?

Nowadays, the United Nations Environmental Programme has begun to assess the environmental effects of war, beginning with the Gulf War in 1991 and continuing with the Kosovo assault by NATO in 1999. When this information is made available, and when it is illuminated by the light of mass media, perhaps calculations will begin to factor in the possibilities of environmental collateral damage. Once that happens, it may b harder to sell the concept of war. There is precedence for this kind of progress.

Both the peace movement and the promoters of international humanitarian law point toward the increasing rate of civilian deaths during the 20th century as a function of technology outstripping ethical concerns. Because of the hyperdestructiveness of the weaponry in the arsenals, more damage has accrued to innocent bystanders while the military itself has not sustained as much because it has hardened defenses. Thus, during World War I, approximately 90 percent of the battlefield mortalities were military personnel and 10 percent were civilians struck collaterally (this does not include civilian figures of disease and starvation). The weaponry and policies gradually changed that ratio until, by the end of the war in Vietnam, it was precisely reversed. Ninety percent of the casualties were civilian and it became evermore obvious that war itself was a violation of basic human rights.

Under the bright glare of media scrutiny and the resultant pressure by people, politicians and military began to respond. Now, during the 1999 Kosovo air attacks, we find the civilian deaths at approximately 2,000 and military deaths at approximately 5,000 (as counted by traditional official methods, meaning prompt mortalities). Not only are there far fewer overall deaths than would have been expected just a decade ago from such a massive air assault, but those deaths are mostly military. This is a clear and direct result of the pressure applied to politicians and to the military by concerned citizens.

This tells us to continue this pressure toward defeating the very consideration of war as an alternative in nation-state conflict management. If we can leverage the environment into the decision-makers' calculations will war then be less likely? Will we see the politicians and the military respond with more precision—or less toxic—weapons designed to go a bit easier on the Earth? Conflict management is a process and we all affect public policy. Incremental change is clearly preferable to no change, even though abolition of war and war preparation is the prize upon which we keep our eyes.

NATO attack unravels Balkan ecology

"No one knows," says Erik Torch, "whether the long-range effects of the NATO air war will be worse because of the depleted uranium left there in unknown quantities, or because of the hazardous materials blown up by NATO bombs and released into the air and waters." Torch, a naturalist and a volunteer for the international nongovernmental organization Balkan Peace Team since 1997, lived and worked in Kosovo and Serbia before and after the 1999 attack and visited the US for a few weeks in late 1999, documenting the aftermath of the war in a slide presentation.

The thousands of bombs dropped on Serbia and Kosovo during the 1999 March to May air assault have had serious effects on the environment there. The Joint UNEP/UNCHS Balkans Task Force, a project of the UN in general and the Nairobi-based UNEP and UN Centre for Human Settlements in particular, launched an investigation almost immediately upon the cessation of the bombing campaign. It identified the same areas of concern as mentioned by Erik Torch. Headed by Pekka Haavisto, former Finnish Environment and Development Cooperation Minister, the BTF process involved some 60 experts in environmental assessment drawn from 26 NGOs, 19 nations and six UN agencies. (United: 3)

Results are mixed, then, if we rely on that early UNEP report, but the photos of fuel and chemical depots burning at Pancevo and elsewhere tell a clearly bleak story. In the aftermath of the UNEP report, questions remain. A Belgrade man wrote wondering why, since the bombing, did the sour cherry trees lose all their leaves, put out a second leafing and then lose them all again? He also asked how we can tell the difference between illnesses induced by exposure to various war toxics, such as depleted uranium, and the illnesses that come from the sheer stress of war itself. (Cvijovic) This is the kind of sad state in which war leaves a people.

The UNEP report concluded that Yugoslavia's heaviest war pollution is confined to industrial cities. Site investigations by teams of UN scientists found no evidence of widespread or long-term catastrophe. But UNEP urged the Yugoslavia government to immediately clean up several "hot spots." One is in Pancevo, where NATO strikes on oil refineries, petrochemical plants and fertilizer factories released mercury and other carcinogens over the ground and into the 1.2-mile-long canal leading to the Danube. Another major problem is a brew of poisonous waste, including dioxin and polychlorinated biphenyls (PCBs), leaking from the Zastava car factory in Kragujevac.

This contamination poses a "serious threat to human health," according to Pekka Haavisto, a former Finnish environment minister and head of the UNEP team in charge of the Balkans. (Fleishman)

Looking at the actual photos and reading real-time email messages from civilians in Belgrade during the attacks, those documents belie the official position that the air war was not necessarily an environmental disaster. Numerous civilian accounts of thick, choking clouds of noxious smoke cannot be ignored or dismissed by any greenwashed report. Environmentalists simply point to the visible effects, especially in the industrial cities, with toxic chemicals in their depots struck both intentionally and accidentally and then dispersed widely by the winds of war. Indeed, some scientists predict it will be decades before ecosystems recover from the thousands of tons of toxic chemicals threatening water supplies and contaminating fields.

"Our mountains are packed with war waste and bomb fragments," said Vojislav Vasic, an antigovernment scientist and president of Yugoslavia's Natural Museum in Belgrade. "Tons of mercury—like an environmental time bomb—have settled at the bottom of the Danube. These consequences are not spectacular or easy to see right now. But they are quiet ones that will be with us for years." (Fleishman)

Official findings provide the international community with planning tools for future post-conflict realities. Will the cost-benefit calculation on the decision to go to war change? There is general doubt, however, that the BTF report truly did much more than scratch the surface of the environmental consequences of the war. The value of the UNEP study, then, may actually be counterproductive.

The BTF report highlighted four areas of immediate environmental concern: Pancevo, Kragujevac, Novi Sad and Bor.

Debris in the Danube and mercury in the ground around Pancevo, decontamination of dioxin and PCB hotspots around Kragujevac, remediation of water in Novi Sad and sulfur dioxide pollution at Bor are identified problems. Some of the concern was due to the Kosovo War, and some was caused by lack of environmental enforcement by the Federal Republic of Yugoslavia .

Pollution respects no boundaries, naturally, so border-state Romania remains alarmed by the airborne and riverborne war damage to the environment. A June 1999 report from the Romanian Ministry of Waters, Forests and Environmental Protection indicated that no major air or water pollution had been detected to date. But the Romanian authorities acknowledged that a low level of persistent pollution had been discovered by monitoring devices, and its long term effect still needs to be determined. (Savulescu)

The Ministry of Waters, Forests and Environmental Protection (MWFEP) report states that the main environmental problems caused by the Yugoslav war are heavy metal concentrations in the Danube River water and acid rains in Romania's southwestern counties, Timis and Caras-Severin. (Savulescu)

Routine and special water analyses indicated concentrations above the maximum permitted levels of heavy metals such as copper, chrome, cadmium, lead and zinc in several Danube River areas, such as the Portile de Fier Romanian-Yugoslav dam. A peak level of 55 times the allowable level of zinc was determined on April 23, 1999. Phenol concentrations over the maximum legal level have also been determined. (Savulescu)

Like refugees fleeing before the ravages of war and trampling the environment as they are pushed away, and just as the fear and hatred crosses borders in the wake of war, so too, the pollution caused by battle strikes affects entire populations who can only wish they had nothing to do with the war begun by others. If we live on Earth, war anywhere is *our* problem everywhere.

sources

Canby, Thomas Y., "After the Storm," *National Geographic*, 180:2, August 1991 (2-32)

Congressional Quarterly, ***The Middle East, Ninth Edition***. Washington DC: CQ Press, 2000.

Cvijovic, Drasko, e-mail, 1 November 1999.

Earth Island Institute, "War Is a Waste," factsheet, 1991.

Environmental News Service, "Danube River ecosystem caught in Balkan War," 7 May 1999, http://ens.lycos.com/ens/may99/1999L-05-07-05.html

Environmental News Service, "Environmental damage assessed in Kosovo, Serbia," 23 July 1999, http://ens.lycos.com/ens/jul99/1999L-07-23-03.html

Fleishman, Jeffery, "Yugoslavia is afloat in 'war waste,'" *The Philadelphia Inquirer*, 14 October 1999.

National Public Radio, late March 1999.

Pope, Carl, "War on Earth," *Sierra*, May/June 1991: 54-58.

Thomas, William, ***Bringing the War Home***. Anchorage AK: Earthpulse Press Incorporated, 1998.

Thomas, William, ***Scorched Earth: The Military's Assault on the Environment***. Gabriola Island, Vancouver, British Columbia: New Society Press, 1995.

Torch, Erik, eyewitness account, presented in Duluth MN, 8 November 1999.

Savulescu, Alexandru R., "Romania Assesses War Related Eco-Damage, "Environmental News Service, http://ens.lycos.com/ens/jun99/1999L-06-04-03.html

United Nations Environment Programme, ***The Kosovo Conflict: Consequences for the Environment & Human Settlements***. Nairobi, Kenya: UNEP, 1999.

Human flood: refugees flee before war

"We were told: 'You are refugees.' We didn't know that there was a name for being in another country."
– Mayan native from northern Guatemala (Falla: 178)

My mother is translating, her voice shakes. "he says that if anyone else tries to commit murder or suicide, she will be shot, and that we will all be shot too."...She pauses and the soldier shouts some more. "He says we have to understand that they do not like killing. He says that if anyone tries to kill anyone, they will shoot all of us."
– Agate Nesaule, WW II refugee (Nesaule: 79)

When the hail of bullets and rain of bombs begin, the flood of targeted humanity gathers and soon starts to run. Like so many other human-caused phenomena, refugee flight was not a real environmental problem when the Earth was a sea of wilderness dotted with islands of human disturbance. Now, however, the situation is reversed and the oceans of humanity cause serious damage when whipped up by the storms of war. This has not been a mere side effect of armed human conflict; the wall of displaced humanity rolls over a countryside not as a ripple effect but as a tidal wave of great and destructive force. Like any flood, the fresh becomes the dirty, the clean becomes the unhealthy and entire habitats are swallowed up in diseased destruction. Beautiful little children and caring women—the main channel of most rivers of war refugees—become part of cholera-producing, typhus-carrying, eco-trampling, resource-gobbling waves of misery. Often, they precipitate even more conflict, in a kind of mutually-reinforcing dynamic of tragedy.

Refugees from war and other causes will drive the world toward more war. "Scarcities can reduce or constrain economic productivity to the detriment of both local communities and larger regional and national economies. Affected people, who are usually already economically and ecologically marginal, may migrate or be expelled to other rural lands or cities. These migrants often trigger group-identity (usually interethnic) conflicts when they move to new areas, and local decreases in wealth can cause insurgencies and rebellion." (Homer-Dixon: 133) Thus, the refugee issue belongs in our consideration both as a result *and* a cause of war, an ecological disaster that follows *and* often precedes violent group conflict.

At the end of 1994, more than 27 million war refugees and people displaced by war marked an increase of elevenfold since 1970. From Burma to Rwanda, from Somalia to Afghanistan, the tremendous numbers add up to half a percent of humanity, nearly one in every 200 of us on Earth. (United: 26) More than 90 percent of the armed conflict since World War II, despite the high profile interstate shooting wars, has been internal. While bombs, bullets and landmines have taken a tremendous toll, the direct cut-off of food and potable water has taken an even greater toll in those conflict areas. In the conflict zones, more than 100 million people are chronically malnourished. (United: 24) Even in zones of poverty, the costs to women and children are greatly multiplied by war. Contrast, for example, the crushing poverty in part of South Asia not currently experiencing a shooting war. The rate of under-five mortality is 120 per thousand. It is 175 per thousand in Sub-Saharan Africa, but in areas not only poor but impacted by recent shooting wars in Afghanistan, Angola, Mozambique and Sierra Leone, the under-five mortality rate is more than 250 per thousand. (United: 26) Though no one will be arrested as culpable, this is a giant war crime, an offense against innocent humanity. The United Nations Development Programme says this about the positive feedback loop (reciprocal causation, or mutually reinforcing dynamic) of war and poverty:

> *The connection between conflict and human development runs both ways. Years of internal warfare undermine standards of human development. And long periods of neglect of human development, especially for particular racial or ethnic groups, can eventually provoke violent conflicts.* (United: 26)

What makes this so bitter and protracted so often is that the conflicts that produce war and refugees are frequently about seemingly non-negotiable issues, such as group identity or even group survival. (Harik: 384)

One of our most recent, visible examples was the eruption of Kosovar Albanian refugees immediately upon the beginning of the air attack in the spring of 1999 in the Balkans. The first sorties flew on 24 March and by 28 March two main streams of persecuted Kosovar Albanians were on the move toward the northern Albanian border and the Kosovo-Montenegro crossings. Some 18,500 frightened souls pushed north and another 7,000 toward Montenegro's checkpoints at Podgorica and Rozaje. (Fleishman: 1A)

And that was just the first wash of weary victims. The initial trickles had been steadily flowing out of Kosovo as the Serbian minority began their ethnic cleansing campaign, which was itself in response to the guerrilla attacks by the Kosovo Liberation Army starting in late winter of 1998. During the ensuing year, Kosovar Albanians left their homes and homeland in a small but desperate stream. Ironically, this exodus was the justification used by NATO to bomb Kosovo, precipitating the major catastrophic outwash of refugees that was the hallmark of the war on the ground. The Serbian Christians wanted the Kosovar Albanian Muslims out, and were provided the justification for acting on that desire by the NATO attacks. Such is the logic and effect of war in one permutation or another. When one's only tool is a gun, every problem begins to look like a menacing target; NATO was never designed to negotiate. They are a military alliance and, with the fall of the Soviet Union, had nothing but planetary ostracism to deter them. That wasn't nearly strong enough to prevent them from waging the disastrous campaign against the Serbs and the collaterally damaged Kosovar Albanians. Both peoples paid a dear price for the "help." Disregarded almost entirely in the short run, as ever, is the environment. Refugees are always annihilatory on ecological subsystems. It's all quite predictable and, sure enough, it wasn't long before communicable diseases, and diseases caused by lack of sanitation, were prevalent amongst the great moving floods and subsequently encamped reservoirs of the displaced.

This particular situation was exploited ferociously by the media of the attacking nations with no sense of irony whatever. Reports of thousands of bomb attacks from 30,000 feet in the air were accompanied by photos of truckloads of sweatered children and scarved grandmothers exposed to the winter weather, plastic-sheeted lean-to's, and even an ailing aged grandmother in a wheelbarrow being pushed by a strong but exhausted young Kosovar Albanian man.

As in so many other wartorn borderlands, Albania was scarcely able to handle this outpouring of humanity in flight, most without possessions or resources. As the poorest country in Europe with just 3 million citizens, what could beleaguered Albania do in the face of hundreds of thousands of the poorest and most destitute of all, the war refugees? "It's hell up there now," was the humanitarian assessment. At that point, with a half million refugees from the previous year and 100,000 in estimated exodus, the UN had housing for 4,000 and NATO had made no provisions whatsoever. (Fleishman: 7A) Like locusts in the winds of war, the victims became the attack on the land and waters even as bombed and burning chemical factories became the scourge of the atmosphere.

Emigration is obviously not always a result of shooting wars; there are millions of people moving for a wide variety of reasons. The UN estimates that some 150 million citizens of Earth have left their homes—2.5 percent of all people on the planet. (Chapin: 38) But the problem of war refugees became worse, rather than better, in the final quarter of the 20th century. In the early 1960s, the number of international refugees was estimated at a bit more than 1 million. (Renner, 1997: 124) 1976 figures from the United Nations High Commissioner for Refugees reported 2.8 million international refugees and that figure swelled to nearly 19 million by 1993. (Chapin: 38) By 1997 the river of war refugees had diminished a bit to a still-high number of 13.6 million. (Chapin: 38) But the total number of international refugees from all causes had risen to 27.4 million by 1995. This reflects *only* the international refugees. The intranational populations in flight from armed conflict, the domestic or internal refugees, numbered an estimated 50 million, according to 1998 UNHCR tallies, and some put the figure as high as 90 million. (Renner, 1997: 124) Like a giant tipping tub, the sloshing inevitably spills over across borders, making nearly every civil war the business of all neighboring nations and of the entire UN. To throw burning oil on the tidal waves of the displaced, guerrilla forces will often travel with, or parallel to, these great groups of wanderers, threatening to draw pursuing troops with them across borders, thus widening wars. And often the guerrilla will use the refugee camps as sympathetic safe zones, arranging arms deals right under the noses of authorities and further endangering the people they claim they are liberating or protecting.

Not really a direct problem for the wealthy nations under most circumstances, the vast majority of these refugees only make it to the poor bordering countries. Just 16 percent arrive in Europe or North America; the remaining 84 percent land in Africa (36 percent), the Middle East (33 percent) and in South and Central Asian nations (11 percent). (Chapin: 39) An astonishing 63 percent of the population of Liberia are refugees, 45 percent of Rwanda and Bosnia, and the figure is 20 percent for Afghanistan. (Renner, 1997: 125) This flies in the face of rich northern nation protectionist, closed-border diatribes, which reveal wellsprings of resentment. Certainly the numbers of refugees entering wealthy nations are certainly not insignificant, just minor by comparison. Refugees are persecuted north and south, albeit usually far worse closer to their homelands. Violence perpetrated against, for example, Turkish immigrants to Germany, pales alongside the violence that all-too-often accompanies the crowds of fleeing civilians and guerrilla forces in the periphery nations.

While xenophobia is regrettable and a cause of conflict, it is also a *result* of atrocities committed during conflict (or the credible rumors thereof) and not without its miserable logic. When, for example, Rwandan refugees fled to the Congo, they were met by violence based on fear of genocidal assaults precedented by recent history. Citizens naturally fear widening war coming their way with the foot-weary or waterlogged in flight. Thus, when Vietnamese boatloads of refugees wandered desperately into Malaysian waters, that government rejected them, even as leaky vessels sank. (Chapin: 41) The story is similar from India to Fiji, from Africa to Iran.

Jordan, a nation known in recent years for adroit juggling of crisis and conflict without resort to war, had to again prove its capabilities under extreme duress immediately following the Gulf War. To imagine the impact of the returning Jordanians and Palestinians—evicted from Kuwait following the war—visualize the crisis if the US were forced to embrace a sudden increase of 30 million in one year, the proportional equivalent to Jordan's 12 percent growth due to immigration of war refugees. (Elhance: 95) The relatively few immigrants allowed into the US annually raises periodic outbursts of extreme debate; what if a country like Jordan were to be so closed? We would see an extraordinary rise in conflict, perhaps even additional wars. Thus, xenophobia works in both ways, to cause conflict by failing to yield to the immense pressure of a would-be migrant population pressing borders, and to cause conflict by its application to a migrant group once inside foreign borders. As immigrants constringe surplus stocks of survival goods, so too is goodwill squeezed out of the host people, unless international help is serious and sustained.

One of the most opportunistic and cynical treatments of refugees is to turn them into proxy troops, as the US did first to Cubans fleeing Castro and two decades later to Somocistas running from Sandinistas in Nicaragua. Comparably, Bangladeshi civilians in flight from civil war in the early 1970s were armed by the Indian government and sent against Pakistan just as Afghanis seeking refuge were given guns and propelled against the Soviets. The Russians did the same to Chechens in flight from Grosny in 1999. Palestinians have historically been trained and armed by Arab states to fight Israel (Chapin: 45) and Kurds have been used with little regard by both Iran and Turkey, against each other.

Can we always determine the definition, cause and effect of people driven to leave home? When they form a photographable human river from a shooting zone to anywhere else, they are clearly a result of dangerous conflict. But when they trickle toward a pool from a million sources, the phenomenon is less obvious. However, as a further attack on the environment, as another causal factor in crowding and consequential poor health conditions, approximately 20-30 million people worldwide continue to relocate from rural to urban areas annually, adding to scarcity issues and thus to potential conflict. (Renner, 1997: 125) Economic refugees can create conditions that lead to war refugees.

Compounding the problems of refugee movement is the ecological and economic lack of skill when demobilization succeeds the peace accord; the various armed factions cannot farm with much skill any longer, especially if the war has gone on for the decades we've seen all too often. They know how to make their living with their weapons and everyone is telling them to stop carrying the only tools they know how to use. Not only are they losing face by picking up a hoe and laying down the AK, they don't know what to do with that hoe any longer. Making war has taught them to abuse the land, not care for it. They have learned that the highest value is destruction and now they are being forced to literally stoop to encourage delicate life. "Most of them did not have any profession...and now—in a disarmed situation...the only thing that they know how to do is to kill." So said Graca Machel, Mozambican children's rights spokesperson and widow of Mozambican president Samora Machel. (Sutherland: 118)

We need only look at the examples of attempted or temporary demobilization—Afghanistan, Angola, Cambodia—to see the hardball facts: declaring peace or a ceasefire is not enough. Even in Nicaragua and El Salvador, where demobilization was completed, reintegration has been as fragile as reëducation has been insufficient. (Renner, 1995: 155) From Liberia to Uganda to Chad to Mozambique, the war may be over, cantonment may be called complete, but the land is still suffering from the mines and other dangers while the former army or guerrilla are reluctantly learning to make an honest living. Many are eager for the swashbuckling days of parading with weaponry, of feeling powerful in a frightening time, and generally being the indolent recipients of everyone else's tedious farm and factory labor. They often do a poor job tilling the land and care not for it. Soil exhaustion, erosion and over-chemicalization are the marks of a former military man behind the tractor, spray rig or even hoe. As the ecology continues to unravel, so does the peace accord signed in hope. (Renner, 1995: 155)

Global initiatives to slow and stop small arms transfers are one hopeful sign; when these weapons are fewer so are the casualties and the subsequent wave of refugees. A major effort to shift national and international budgets from militaries to humanitarian assistance and sustainable development will also offer a pillar of hope. The refugee problem is so widespread and so deep that it will require widespread sacrifice and deep commitment to resolve. It will also take time, a luxury the starving babies don't have. Thus the urgency.

sources

Chapin, Wesley D., "Immigration and Security: A Review of ***The Global***

Migration Crisis: Challenge to States and to Human Rights by Myron Weiner," *1999-2000 Journal for the Study of Peace and Conflict*, Stevens Point WI: Wisconsin Institute for Peace and Conflict Studies, 1999-2000. (36-53).

Elhance, Arun P., ***Hydropolitics in the 3rd World: Conflict and Cooperation in International River Basins***. Washington DC: United States Institute of Peace, 1999.

Falla, Ricardo, ***Massacres in the Jungle: Ixcán, Guatemala, 1975-1982***. Boulder CO: Westview Press, 1994.

Fleishman, Jeffrey, and Lori Montgomery, "Refugees adding to region's instability," (including AP photos) *Duluth News-Tribune,* Knight Ridder, 29 March 1999: 1A & 7A.

Harik, Judith P. "The Effects of Protracted Social Conflict on Resettlement of the Displaced in Postwar Lebanon," in ***Conflict Resolution in the Arab World: Selected Essays***, Paul Salem, editor. Beirut, Lebanon: American University of Beirut, 1997.

Homer-Dixon, Thomas F., ***Environment, Scarcity, and Violence***. Princeton NJ: Princeton University Press, 1999.

Nesaule, Agate, ***A Woman in Amber: Healing and Trauma of War and Exile***. NYC: Penguin Books, 1995.

Renner, Michael, "Budgeting for Disarmament," in: Worldwatch Institute, ***State of the World 1995***. New York: W.W. Norton & Company Ltd., 1995: 150-169.

Renner, Michael, "Transforming Security," in: Worldwatch Institute, ***State of the World 1997***. New York: W.W. Norton & Company Ltd., 1997: 115-131.

Sutherland, Bill and Matt Meyer, ***Guns and Gandhi in Africa: Pan African Insights on Nonviolence, Armed Struggle and Liberation in Africa***. Trenton NJ: Africa World Press, Inc, 2000.

Section Three: Ecological Causes of Conflict

> *Convinced that the global spread of AIDS is reaching catastrophic dimensions, the Clinton administration has formally designated the disease for the first time as a threat to U.S. national security that could topple foreign governments, touch off ethnic wars and undo decades of work in building free-market democracies abroad.* (Gellman: 1A)

> *I believe that in coming decades the world will probably see a steady increase in the incidence of violent conflict that is caused, at least in part, by environmental scarcity. Developing countries are likely to be affected sooner and more severely than developed countries...they often do not have the financial, material, and human capital resources to buffer themselves from the effects of environmental scarcities; and their economic and political institutions tend to be fragile and riven with discord.*
>
> –Thomas Homer-Dixon, ***Environment, Scarcity, and Violence*** (Homer-Dixon, 1999: 4)

On 6 April 1994, Rwandan president Juvenal Habyarimana was killed—likely assassinated by coup plotters—in a mid-flight explosion. His Hutu loyalists launched a bloody campaign of genocide that murdered between half a million and a million Tutsis in a three month period. The world watched an ethnic bloodbath. There was no popular examination of any other motive.

But the populace was locked into a situation undercut by explosive population growth, increasingly cramped and degraded land, the inevitable resultant food shortages, and a legacy of post-colonial tribal favoritism and the discrimination lingering painfully between peoples.

(Renner: 115) The admixture comprises a set of contributory and—with the assassination—sufficient *casus belli* to precipitate a horrendous war. Without the economic and ecologic suffering, would such a slaughter have occurred? It is extremely doubtful. Peace researcher Michael Andregg notes that there is a "simple relationship between competition for resources and the probability of war," and he describes the line of the graph plotting that relationship as monotonic and detectable by correlations. (Andregg: 47) University of Toronto researcher Thomas Homer-Dixon asserts that "civil violence in Chiapas, South Africa, Pakistan, the Philippines, and Haiti cannot be properly understood or explained without taking into account the causal role of environmental scarcity." (Homer-Dixon, 1999: 7) Ancient enemies can long simmer with hatred for each other, but a good outbreak of hunger can be the gasoline waiting for the eventful match to be tossed onto ethnic tension, transmogrifying it into ethnic conflagration. As Eritrea and Ethiopia go to war yet again in May 2000, Kofi Annan tells them that their famine may be drought-induced but that the starvation will only increase with more war.

Essentially, we have a war system that is on the make around the world, after more resources, both natural and human, in order to convert those resources to power and, in turn, that power back into the ability to control more resources. Fiction writer Kurt Vonnegut called such a system, "Idiot's Delight," presumably meaning that the expenditure of one in search of the other has so many negative consequences that it takes a clever mind, but an ethical idiot, to play it. When artificially created shortages are no longer artificial but all too real, we can expect a rise in acute conflict. (Homer-Dixon, 1991, part 1: 2)

Though an arms manufacturer would not use any definition of the word "security" that is not arsenal-related, the first victims of these tragic outbreaks of violence are calling for a new definition of that term.

> *War and preparation for war reduce and destroy resources and limit and complicate the conditions for care and nurture. Women who bring forth human life, and carry the responsibility for maintaining it and providing it with the most humane quality possible, see security in terms of the possibilities for life, its maintenance, and the improvement of its quality. Security lies in things hoped for and planned for, perhaps more than in things as they are. Security is in large part* **futures perception.** — Betty Reardon (Reardon: 21-22)

Thus Reardon and other feminist scholars and activists make a deceptively simple yet elegant primary security requisite, that "our planet will continue to be able to sustain life." Reardon hones in on the core of the connections from conflict to human rights to the environment, noting along the way that building and maintaining arsenals "are destroying natural systems" and that the "very weapons we have developed to defend our security are themselves a threat to our security in the potential consequences of their use in combat and in the actual processes of their development and testing." (Reardon: 23) This nexus will only be analyzed with difficulty, but if we can peel back the causal layers of the conflict onion, we can cook up some solutions.

The causes of any event may be analyzed in terms of "necessary," "contributory," and "sufficient." That is, it is *necessary* for a nation to have atomic weapons in order to wage nuclear war. It is always *necessary* for social mores to admit a collective violent defense for there to be any war. Extreme water shortage in a downstream nation may be a *contributory factor*—that is, a factor that itself probably wouldn't produce an interstate shooting war, but would contribute to rising tensions—and the level of contribution to the likelihood of outbreak is variable. Some combination of necessary and contributory factors will produce the *sufficient* conditions at some point, and violence will break out.

Historian Paul Kennedy describes the war system as the prime motivator for the outreach and grasp of all empires. He recounts, for example, mid-18th century English activities of the early Industrial Age, clutching after resources in India, West Africa and eastern North America in an effort to simultaneously pay for her war with France and subsidize Prussia for its part in what would become the Seven Years War. These tremendous financial burdens were only possible because the armies made it possible to raid the natural bounty of nations elsewhere. "Here," writes Kennedy, "was an excellent example of profit being converted into power, and of British sea power being used (e.g., in the West Indies) for national profit." (Kennedy: 113) Idiot's delight.

The conflicts inherent in the injustice of colonial domination continue to haunt much of the so-called developing world—a world that some correctly call "maldeveloped." Or, as Ivan Illich notes, development is effected at a direct cost to subsistence. Quite simply, all the tribal and indigenous peoples of the world were well-developed into their ecological addresses—their habitats, their niches—until the technologically dominating invaders stole their land, their human work power, and as a result, their integrity as a people. Satirical peace poet Hilaire Belloc finished one poem about this conquest by noting, "*Whatever happens, we have got, the Maxim gun, and they have not*," that gun being an early machine gun for use in terrorizing bow-and-arrow hunter-gatherers.

Those early peoples were lost to history and to our analysis for a long period. We are finally beginning to realize what they offer to us; anthropologist Margaret Mead showed scientifically that we are not bound to kill because we are hard-wired to do so, but that models existed that combined peace and a greater depth of true security. Patricia M. Mische, in a powerful 1989 piece of war and peace system exegesis, notes that feminist values—decentralized leadership, care for the land and a non-hierarchical equality amongst societal members—were part and parcel of both general peace and ecological stability in prehistoric times. (Mische: 298-301) As armies and empires moved across the globe, the male-dominated war system replaced that ecofeminist model, bringing war and wasted land.

As the indigenous lands of the world were plundered, the Spanish, English, Dutch, French and Portuguese imperial rulers made increasing attempts to mitigate the costly wars between and amongst themselves. One such attempt was the Pope's early declaration of the division of the entire world between Spain and Portugal, a pronouncement of such arrogance and irrelevance that it was shaken off in most quarters immediately. Another such "peace" process transpired in the winter of 1884-1885 in Berlin, where the Great Powers met to cut up and parcel out Africa. The primary players were France, England and Germany; the US and Russia were regarded as second-rate observers at that time. New borders were drawn, agreements were made, and peace between the Great Powers was achieved for the moment. It wouldn't be for another 30 years that Europe would tear itself apart and another 20 before doing it again, ruining its colonial hold over the rest of the world due in part to its inability to achieve agreement amongst themselves. (Kennedy: 194)

By 1900, the United Kingdom stretched around the world, from East to West, from North to South. Canada dominated their holdings in the West, with British Guiana and the Falkland Islands as outposts in South America and a few islands in the Caribbean. Africa was slashed up by the various Europowers and the UK was left holding a ring of African nations from Gambia and Sierra Leone, Gold Coast and Nigeria, south to Rhodesia and Cape Province and back north to Egypt and Sudan. Across the Gulf, the UK held Aden and huge amounts of Asia from India, Ceylon, Singapore and Hong Kong to Australia and New Zealand. (Kennedy: 225) The environments of these lands were being sliced open and gutted at tremendous rates to make it possible for the empire to exist. The other Europowers were doing the same on smaller but still quite significant scales.

The imperiousness of what Europe did to Africa, the Americas and Asia continues to redound on the peoples who live in nation-states that were unnaturally stitched together—or, in the case of some nations, rent apart—by Europeans from the 15th century onward, all in search of more natural resources with which to build and maintain empires. Thus is revealed a positive feedback loop of land grabbing, resource extraction, armament building and more heavily armed land grabbing, *ad finitum* to the ends of the Earth. This will take a long time indeed to shake out. This is what still drives resource wars, wars over the environment. This is what we often call ethnic war nowadays. In many ways, because of the concomitant tampering with national-tribal borders and theft of the environmental basis for indigenous economies, these are two sides to the same coin.

Related and gaining in prominence now is the deterioration of the environment through pollution of natural resources. This degradation makes even local self-reliance more and more difficult as desertification and water pollution deprive entire peoples of their ability to survive, let alone thrive.

It is clear that in the post-Cold War world, as interstate armed conflict diminishes and intrastate shooting wars break out with increased frequency and ferocity, we are called to a deeper understanding of the interplay between the quality of the environment and what it provides—or no longer provides—for the people who live there. When we understand the environmental causes and correlatives to war as well as the environmental costs of war and war preparation, we can begin to see a much larger yet more accurately detailed picture of the current war system. This perspective is critical to the development of a peace system vision.

It will also take patience. When Robert Mugabe calls the white farmers of his nation, Zimbabwe, "the enemy," and supports the March-April 2000 takeovers of their lands by black war veterans, he is alienating the whites of the North. When he fails to denounce the murder of some of those white farmers, he is certainly driving that alienation deeper. When he then calls for Britain to pay for it all—to compensate the thousands of white farmers who are being forced out of their homes and off their farms—he just about finishes off the job of poor public relations with the white citizenry of the North. Yet, he is correct and justifiable at so many levels, and his countrypeople's grievances are indeed long-standing and unresolved. Though they are, by any civilized standards, straying into negative means in order to achieve some overdue justice, they cannot be credibly be judged by societies that plan for and execute massive killing campaigns from 30,000 feet, also in the name of effecting justice. What is shifting and settling out in Zimbabwe is all part of the aftermath of colonialism and its environmental-economic impacts.

"Today," writes Michael Renner of the Worldwatch Institute, "humanity is facing a triple security crisis: the effects of environmental decline, the repercussions of social inequality and stress, and the dangers arising out of an unchecked arms proliferation that is a direct legacy of the cold war period." (Renner: 116) We might add the latest recognized contributory factor to war, AIDS, pandemic in Africa, spreading globally, lowering life expectancy dramatically in some nations. This fuels instability and is cited in a January 2000 US National Intelligence Estimate as a serious cause of failed states and the rise of rebel factions. The troops and guerrilla themselves contribute to the spread of the disease, as they are mobile and sexually active.

The links between militarism and a decline in human standards of living represent a mutually reinforcing positive feedback loop of ever more negative results, more injustice and more misery for more people.

Here is the touchstone:
Whom do you get along with?
Who are those who criticize you?
Who are those who do not accept you?
Who are those who flatter you?
Know from that what Christ said once:
"I have come not to bring peace, but division."
There will be division even in the same family,
because some want to live more comfortably
by the world's principles,
those of power and money.
– Archbishop Oscar Romero, 13 November 1977 (Romero: 9)

Only by a breakthrough strategy of disarmament and radical nonviolent intervention in conflict can this cycle of greed ↦ theft ↦ scarcity ↦ war ↦ destruction ↦ more scarcity ↦ conflict be curtailed. It is a philosophical difference that applies equally to ecological conflict and law enforcement. Some favor retributive justice, which incarcerates, punishes and even kills those found to be culpable. Others favor rehabilitative and restorative justice, which may also incarcerate, but which attempts a healing process valuing more life, not less. A grasp of the factors in front of us is a prerequisite to such effective restorative, breakthrough action. What are the primary resource and ecological elements of incipient and ongoing conflict globally and locally?

There are endless categories. There is the depletion and contamination of renewables, including water, wood and food crops. There is overpopulation, overconsumption and unfair distribution of both renewable and unrenewable resources. There is oil and its false promise of high carrying capacity. The extractions and resource captures are all made possible by huge threatening arsenals, quickly transported by the oil so jealously guarded. These are themselves interrelated, of course, and often parts of these are in feedback loops with each other. A large-scale resource extraction project or energy generation project, for example, can also create environmental refugees and fuel tensions between elite distant owners and local indigenous peoples. The owners are invariably well represented in government and the native peoples are historically poor in money but rich in local self-sufficiency based on sustainable use of the environment. Thus the seeds of much "ethnic conflict." The equation in the Middle East truly seems to be that the Pentagon needs to defend its own fuel source by any means at its disposal, as we will discuss in coming chapters.

sources

Andregg, Michael, ***On the Causes of War***. Minneapolis MN: Ground Zero Minnesota, 1996.

Gellman, Barton, "Clinton designates AIDS a threat to U.S. national security," *Duluth News-Tribune* (*Washington Post*), 1 May 2000: 1A.

Homer-Dixon, Thomas F., ***Environment, Scarcity, and Violence***. Princeton NJ: Princeton University Press, 1999.

Homer-Dixon, Thomas F., "On the Threshold: Environmental Changes as Causes of Acute Conflict," *International Security* 16:2 (Fall 1991) (76-116) reprinted on Thomas F. Homer-Dixon website in three parts plus endnotes.

Kennedy, Paul, ***The Rise and Fall of the Great Powers: Economic Change and Military Conflict from 1500 to 2000***. NYC: Random House, 1987.

Mische, Patricia M., "Women, Men, and Systems of Security: From a War System toward a Just Peace System?" in: Ringler, Dick, et al., editors, ***Dilemmas of War and Peace: A Sourcebook***. Madison WI: University of Wisconsin, 1993.

Reardon, Betty, ***Women and Peace: Feminist Visions of Global Security***. Albany NY: State University of New York Press, 1993.

Renner, Michael, "Transforming Security," in: Worldwatch Institute, ***State of the World 1997***. New York: W.W. Norton & Company Ltd., 1997: 115-131.

Romero, Oscar, ***The Violence of Love***. Farmington PA: The Plough Publishing House, 1998 (original 1988, Harper & Row Publishers)

Hydropolitics: water wars and the thirst for justice

We are all sprung from earth and water.
—Xenophanes of Colophon, mid-sixth century B.C.E.

Whiskey is for drinking; water is for fighting over.
—Mark Twain

When we image a peaceful, bubbling flow of clean water over rounded stone we find ancient comfort and soothing relief. Clear, drinkable water is the fluid of life, the balm and salve for the wounds of strife. There is no more sanctified, calming vision in our collective emotional mind and spirit. There is a world of it. It is the lifeblood of Mother Earth.

Said the Teacher to his kinsman: "What is all this quarrel about, Great King?"

"We do not know, Reverend Sir."

"Who then would be likely to know?"

"The commander-in-Chief of the army would be likely to know."

The Commander-in-Chief of the army said, "The Viceroy would be likely to know."

Thus the Teacher put the question first to one and then to another, asking the slave labourers last of all. The slave labourers replied, "The quarrel is about water, Sir."

Then the Teacher asked the King, "How much is water worth, Great King?"

"Very little, Reverend Sir."

"How much are the Khattiyas (warriors) worth, Great King?"

"Khattiyas are beyond price, Reverend Sir."

> *"It is not fitting that because of a little water you should destroy Khattiyas who are beyond price."*
>
> –Dhammapada Commentary, Pali text (Miall: 65)

Water is worth more now than it was in the days of the Dhammapada Commentary. But haven't we also named humans—warriors or not—worth even more than when they were "priceless"? Isn't the formula still the same?, i.e., water for blood is a very poor equation. And the fight itself ruins the equation. From the wars of the ancient Lagash and Umma 4,500 years ago over improper and illegal water theft for irrigation (Gleick: 125), to the modern "Milagro Bean Field Wars" that are fought on a small and large basis, we are sometimes prepared to kill, and certainly to wage conflict, over too little fresh pure water or too much polluted or salt water.

War pollutes water. Indeed, the mere preparation for war, with all its manufacturing requirements and resultant Superfund sites, pollutes water. And the scarcity of clean water pollutes the progress toward peace. Doctors and survivalists alike note that humans can live much longer without food than without water; the urgency of clean water for our survival is powerful, undeniable. Hydropolitics is colored by strong emotion based on a universal sense of entitlement, the Right to a Clean Drink of Water. This right, and its attendant or extrapolative rights to crop irrigation and industrial usage, is at the center of the new Resource Wars occupying at least as much focus as oil and strategic or precious minerals—more focus for poor people on water, more focus for rich multinationals on oil and manufacturing. Desertification, soil erosion, deforestation, water scarcity and pollution all factor in the increasing insecurity and international stress over water politics. Sandra Postel of the Worldwatch Institute reminds us of the ancient Inca maxim, "The frog does not drink up the pond in which it lives." (Postel, 1996: 41) Nor, we might add today, does the wise human community use up fresh water by polluting it until it is no longer fresh.

"Socio-economic development is closely related to the ability to manage water resources in the natural environment." (Falkenmark: 85) The secure amount of usable water as it relates to the overall needs of a nation is foundational to water's national security priority. The factors involved are numerous and not limited to: population, efficiency of distribution, industrial draw (which can itself be radically affected by efficiency and trends), agricultural needs (irrigation, efficient or otherwise) and cultural norms—how much water does a person "need"? Basic human needs—eating and drinking—account for about three-quarters of our worldwide water use. (Falkenmark: 87) This means that, except for increases in efficiency, the amount of water we need isn't really too negotiable. We need what we need or we risk dehydration, starvation or malnutrition and the resultant conflict.

On my old globe, I see that at the northeastern end of the Aral Sea, lies Aral'sk, the port city on that body of water within the-then USSR. On my new maps, Aral'sk sits 30 kilometers from the edge of the smaller Aral Sea, a body of water shrunk by 75 percent of its volume, largely due to Soviet cotton irrigation. Now the Aral Sea, once yielding annual fish catches of up to 50,000 tons, is dead. It is on the border of impoverished and polluted Kazakstan and Uzbekistan and offers no sustenance to either. It formerly provided not only fish but the 60,000 jobs that derived from that industry. Those losses are a source of great tension in the region. (Renner: 118) Ironically, conflict resolution theorists tell us that here and elsewhere, it is the reasonable hope for redress that may actually precipitate the manifestation of those simmering, latent conflicts. Hopelessness, contrary to popular understanding, does not lead to demonstrations, riots, confrontations and war. When so many in the human family have no access to clean drinking water, there is a sad and fatalistic acceptance, unless there is a chance that conflict can regain those losses.

overdrawn at the river bank: stopping water wars

> *The renewable resource most likely to stimulate interstate resource war is river water.*—Thomas Homer-Dixon, codirector, Project on Environmental Change and Acute Conflict, University of Toronto (Postel, 1996: 48)

From the Nile to the Jordan to the Euphrates-Tigris, from the Ganges to the Mekong and all the way back to the great Parana-La Plata basin, international conflict is brewing. At times, it brews faster than the chemical concoctions which increasingly cause the transboundary pollution threatening the quality of these waters.

Just as waging war requires cooperation (within each conflictual party), so too does peaceful distribution of water resources (between potentially conflictual parties). "Unilateralism and water don't mix," notes Richard Solomon, United States Institute of Peace director. (Elhance: ix) All too often, the artificial national borders seem to encourage a claim on many of life's necessities that are just passing through. This applies to clean air and to the birds that inhabit it as well as to water and the fish that live there, especially that fresh water flowing down great river basins through more than one nation. That water is ultimately more valuable than oil and increasingly its banks, shorelines, inlets, outlets and wellheads are bristling with armaments to guard it jealously. Indeed, the root of the word "rival" is shared with river and grew from the concept of those living on the same body of flowing water.

Peace Studies professor Thomas F. Homer-Dixon delineates the effort to analyze water conflict by his construction of categories of environmental scarcity conflict. Supply-induced, demand-induced and structural scarcity trace the origins of the problem, while recognizing that in most water conflict there are elements of more than one of these kinds of scarcity at play.

For example, Homer-Dixon calls the struggles over the Jordan River an issue of resource capture. That is, that the quality or quantity of the resource is not only falling but the population is rising, encouraging powerful groups to grab more, thus setting up a potential spiral of conflict. (Homer-Dixon, 1999: 73)

Indeed, the relatively tiny Jordan River system (compared to other major river basins), at roughly 6,500 square miles, includes riparian states Israel, Syria, Lebanon, Jordan and the Palestinian Authority. This hotbed of conflict over identity and resources seems to know no end to the variety of conflicts, resulting in virtually every kind of traditionally recognized category. Though there has clearly been ferocious conflict between Lebanon and Israel, it was not over the waters of the Jordan; Lebanon is blessed with a much more favorable climate and many other hydrological resources. Similarly, Syria and Israel aren't really in conflict over the Jordan River's main tributary, the Yarmuk, since Syria also receives water from the Euphrates, the Tigris and the Orontes. Water is a serious issue between Israel and the Palestinians and between Israel and Jordan. Agreements from 1993 and 1994 are currently in force and questions continue to develop, especially between the Palestinians and Israelis. (Soffer: 121)

Two families living in peace on a small oasis in the desert may find the water supply clean and adequate to maintain health and prosperity. As soon as the total population exceeds the carrying capacity of the oasis, conflict can erupt and each growing family finds a way to blame the other. One family may grab more than its share and keep it by threat of violence. Just so, when various ethnic groups live on a body of water shared by all, the tensions mount as that resource becomes scarce or unusable (*de facto* scarcity), and a sense of injustice is generally felt by all. Early intervention can possibly avoid the ensuing ethnic instability, but more often the conflict spirals into more serious, less resolvable arenas. Thus, ecological difficulty can often spark conflict that becomes labeled "ethnic" but is actually to some degree "ecological."

Postel names the three overarching drivers to war over water: depletion or degradation (fewer resources available to be divided), population growth (more stakeholders in need of a share) and resource distribution (some take or trash more than their share). (Postel, 1996: 47)

The arid Middle East is illustrative of all three. Israel allows Arabs in the occupied West Bank only one-fourth the water usage per capita, with no new Arab irrigation wells drilled since 1967, while Israel has installed more than 30 for Jewish settlers. While Palestinian Israelis watch their gardens wilt for lack of water, many Israelis enjoy their swimming pools and water their lush green lawns all day in the bright desert sun. (Baker) We cannot wonder at the tension and the contribution to anger levels between peoples who experience this ecological and ethnic imbalance. Indeed, water rights were an important element of the September 1995 peace settlement following the famous Yitzak (Rabin) and Yasser (Arafat) handshake. (Postel, 1996: 48)

While water in the arid Mideast may seem like a distant problem, that region was much wetter in antiquity; desertification there is only an augury of what we can expect from what we continue to do. In truth, for example, while Israeli Jews enjoy about four times the water usage rate as their Arab neighbors in the West Bank, they do so at the expense of the aquifers, overpumping them until wells dry up at some depths and worse, some aquifers are infiltrated by sea water from the Mediterranean. At some point, those swimming pools will be filled with salt water—which is what they ought to be right now—but so too will the drinking water, which will not be viable for anyone. All the while, population is growing, from its current six million to a projected 7.5 million Israelis by 2020. (Homer-Dixon, 1999: 74) Indeed, the Jordan basin is projected to demographically explode, with the highest growth rate (71 percent increase by 2025) of any of the world's most disputed river basins. (Postel, 2000: 47) This confluence of pressures is producing the conflict predicted by demographers and ecologists years ago.

damming big basins: damning peace in the valley

The conflict between the White Moors and black Africans living in the Senegal River basin augers ill for how we treat water, the Earth and each other. In Senegal and Mauritania, following the construction of the Manantali Dam, the increasing advantages of hydroelectric generation, crop irrigation and river navigation were grabbed by the White Moors, who forced the relocation of 70,000 black Mauritanians. (Postel, 1996: 48) This is another example of what we might call ethnic ecological conflict.

Other dam projects have caused serious conflict, upheaval, and the flight of refugees. The Farakka Barrage was built by larger India in the late 1960s-early 1970s, under no international agreement, on the Ganges just before it enters Bangladesh. This dam diverts water to the Hooghly River for irrigation and improved navigation, leaving Bangladesh with scarcely a tenth of its normal flow in dry years, when India diverted it most. (Gleick: 118) "There were places that Bangladeshis were driving bullock carts across that great river bed," says Ahmad Karim, negotiator for Bangladesh in that conflict. (Karim) This led to a conflict serious enough to warrant U.N. action at the request of Bangladesh. While Bangladesh made the request for world intervention in 1976, it would be 21 years before a treaty was signed between the two nations over the matter. (Gleick: 118)

In a problem resembling the India and Bangladesh conflict, the Gabcikovo-Nagymoros dam project escalated and intertwined with ethnic conflict between and among Hungary, Slovakia and the Czech Republic. The roots of the situation began with a major Soviet initiative in the 1950s to construct a hydroelectric plant on the Danube. Treaties were pushed through and construction was begun, even in the face of environmental protests by Hungarians. By 1989, the Hungarian government announced its pullout, Czechoslovakia pushed ahead and the ethnic Hungarians in Czechoslovakia increased their ecological opposition. The situation came to a head in October 1992, as Czechoslovakia began diverting the Danube, Hungary protested strongly and they submitted the dispute to the ICJ. Meanwhile, Hungary started to dismantle its section of the dam, the Slovakian government announced its independence on 1 January 1993 and by October had declared its electric plant would be fully generational. The World Court at last ruled in September 1997 that both parties had violated the 1977 treaty and the outcome remains uncertain. (de Nevers: 156-157)

floods and fighting

The world of water is flooded with paradox; when we have too little, we are ready to fight about it. When we have too much, especially when it is the result of someone else's actions, we are also in conflict. As we fail to act to reverse global warming, the Aral Sea example notwithstanding, hydropolitics will also involve a sharp *decrease* in land as the oceans rise. It is estimated that the expected 50 centimeter rise in global sea level will force the 118 million people living in coastal areas at or below sea level to find new homes. In the already unstable subcontinent, Bangladesh—currently the most densely populated nation on Earth—will lose up to 17 percent of its territory, about 25,000 square kilometers. (Renner: 120) If that happens and doesn't precipitate bloody conflict, a miracle is on its way. The sea rises from the south in poor Bangladesh even as fresh water is pulled away from the north. It will take cooperation and human action to avert more ecological conflict in that region and others.

From the horrific floods in February-March 2000 in Mozambique (which, in another twist of war and ecology, loosened thousands of landmines from that stricken nation's soil and re-placed them in unknown and newly dangerous positions), to the predicted loss of 16 percent of Egypt's land to rising sea levels, we fail to address global warming at our collective peril. While Egypt draws more US military aid than any nation except Israel, that fossil-fuel consuming military isn't going to help when the Mediterranean begins to claim the shorelands. Decreasing use of hydrocarbons might slow or even reverse the problem; troops standing at the seashore firing bullets into the advancing waves are unlikely to help. Military might simply cannot dissuade the tide taking land slower but more even more permanently than an Israeli tank division. We don't negotiate with Mother Earth; we respect Her or suffer the natural consequences.

sources

Baker, Carleta, personal communication, 22 January 2000.

de Nevers, Renée, "Slovakia," in Michael E. Brown and Richard N. Rosecrance, editors, ***The Costs of Conflict: Prevention and Cure in the Global Arena***. Lanham MD: Rowman & Littlefield Publishers, Inc., 1999.

Elhance, Arun P., ***Hydropolitics in the 3rd World: Conflict and Cooperation in International River Basins***. Washington DC: United States Institute of Peace, 1999.

Falkenmark, Malin, "Fresh waters as a factor in strategic policy and action," in Westing, Arthur H., editor, ***Global Resources and International Conflict: Environmental Factors in Strategic Policy and Action***. NYC: Oxford University Press, 1986 (85-113).

Gleick, Peter H., ***The World's Water: The Biennial Report of Freshwater Resources 1998 1999***. Washington DC: Island Press, 1998.

Homer-Dixon, Thomas F., ***Environment, Scarcity, and Violence***. Princeton NJ: Princeton University Press, 1999.

Karim, Ahmad, interview, 1 April 2000.

Miall, Hugh, et al., ***Contemporary Conflict Resolution: The Prevention, Management and Transformation of Deadly Conflicts***. Cambridge UK: Polity Press, 1999.

Postel, Sandra, "Forging a Sustainable Water Strategy," in: Worldwatch Institute, ***State of the World 1996***. New York: W.W. Norton & Company Ltd., 1996.

Postel, Sandra, "Redesigning irrigated agriculture," in: Worldwatch Institute, ***State of the World 2000***. New York: W.W. Norton & Company Ltd., 2000.

Renner, Michael, "Transforming Security," in: Worldwatch Institute, ***State of the World 1997***. New York: W.W. Norton & Company Ltd., 1997: 115-131.

Soffer, Aaron, ***Rivers of Fire: The Conflicts Over Water in the Middle East***. Lanham MD: Rowman & Littlefield, 1999.

Westing, Arthur H., editor, ***Global Resources and International Conflict: Environmental Factors in Strategic Policy and Action***. NYC: Oxford University Press, 1986.

Overpopulation & overconsumption: two bombs

Disease and death are abetted by many factors. Yet, of all factors that combine to degrade health, poverty stands out for its overwhelming role. Indeed, WHO has called poverty the world's biggest killer.

—World Resources Institute (World: 14)

Thus we know, if we believe the World Health Organization, that poverty is the world's biggest killer. We must ask, then, what causes poverty? As of October 1999 there are six billion people on Earth; is that the only reason for poverty, starvation and injustice?

1.3 billion of the world's people live on incomes less than $1 per day. (World: 14) Meanwhile, in the US alone, we are spending close to half a trillion dollars each and every year on a combination of :

- the DoD budget, which is a bit more than half of the total at more than $270 billion annually,
- the Veterans' Department budget,
- the portions of the Department of Energy budget that go to producing nuclear weapons and handling military radioactive waste,
- the portion of the National Aeronautics and Space Administration budget that goes toward launching and maintaining military satellites,
- foreign military aid,
- international armed peacekeeping,
- and, finally, the roughly $100 billion annual share of the interest on the national debt that has accrued on the borrowing necessary to pay for the giant military purchases of the past 20 years, primarily of the Reagan Regime. (CDI: 23)

These are all military expenditures, though almost half are to be found in budgets other than DoD. Is that expenditure necessary? Are the world's poor just a regrettable necessity in order to protect our lifestyle, our freedoms, our national sovereignty? And will those poor masses ever start a war to get their share?

Hominids have been evolving for about five million years on Earth, *Homo sapiens* have been evolving speciated for approximately 300,000 years, and we didn't number one billion humans until 1850. (Westing: 2) We then doubled until, by a mere century later, we were more than two billion. By the late 1980s we had grown to a bulging five billion and we are now pegged at six billion, hurtling along in this new millennium toward some kind of date with exponential destiny.

Most agree that the standard of living to which people aspire (the Euro-US middle class) is not attainable by more than two or three billion. (Westing: 2) This scarcity toward a desired lifestyle is a direct driver to conflict, war preparation and even war. But what if we all simply had enough to live?

Many believe that a nation determined to live on a scale affordable by the entire world, yes, even by the six billion of us, will not need nearly the armed might that we require in order to keep the rest of the world from rushing at us in a hungry, diseased, poverty-stricken frenzy. If we would take collective responsibility for our impact on the Earth and take only our share, perhaps we could scale back our national security apparatus to fit the defensive needs of any people; it might even work if we learned robust nonviolence. As it is, we justify our immense outlays by citing such a list of "enemies" as North Korea, Iraq, Iran, Cuba, Libya and Syria. A glancing consideration of these nations reveals basket cases of famine and disease due directly to their misplaced focus on military expenditure, especially the worst of them, North Korea. How the Pentagon and its apologists manage to justify such a theft from the mouths of the hungry is astonishing when one considers that Cuba spends less than $1 billion annually on its military, Iran and Iraq together manage to throw a combined $6 billion down the bombs-and-guns rat hole each year, Syria spends approximately $2 billion on their so-called national defense and starving North Korea misspends $5 billion annually. The total, then, for all these official enemies, is about $15 billion. Compare—or, rather, contrast—that to our Department of Defense budget; you would have to take that enemy aggregate total and multiply it by 17.3 to equal our annual expense just on the Pentagon, not even counting all the extras that are really military funds directed to other departments. (CDI: 29) Thus, even for those who believe that the US ought to be the world's policeman, the weight and freight of this death train ought to give commonsensical pause. Does the police force need to spend 17.3 times what all the criminal organizations *combined* spend? And who, then, polices the police force? It is endless and illimitable if we accept the war system.

The costs of this battological paradigm are both tedious and tremendous. Some of the biggest categories that reflect the suffering due to military activities:

- rudimentary education. Almost a billion adults on this poor planet are illiterate while rulers have spent about $8 trillion developing and maintaining the atomic arsenal that daily threatens all of life. (Sivard, 1996: 5)
- health care funding. Half the governments of the world spend more on their militaries than on an attack on the direct enemies of good health (medicine, sanitation, agricultural development) (Sivard, 1996: 5)
- children's preventive care. During each *minute*, around the Earth, on average, 30 children under the age of five die as a direct result of malnutrition or lack of basic medicine, even as the world misspends $1.4 million on the militaries. (Sivard, 1996: 5)

These are numbing numbers, but the preventable death of a child under five every two seconds amounts to a violation of all our biological imperatives, all our social norms, indeed, all common sense, doesn't it?

That the US spends so much on the military and receives so much profit is no coincidence. It is not divine providence; it is direct theft. It comes not from working harder; it comes from using those weapons to enforce cheap labor and cheap raw materials from the poorest nations.

Understanding relative poverty is also important. The United Nations Human Development Programme notes that, while the average income in Japan, for example, is 36 times the average income in Tanzania, the per capita income of the poorest 20 percent in Japan is 130 times more than that of the poorest 20 percent in Tanzania. (United: 13) Peace researcher Johan Galtung talks about these disparities as setting up natural conflicts between the rich in the poorest countries and that nation's poor even as that wide gulf tends to strengthen bonds between the ruling classes of the rich and poor nations alike. (Barash: 44)

WTO, poverty and conflict

Which brings us to a discussion of what amounts to a new imperialism, the newest trade authorities that usurp national environmental, labor rights and human rights laws. These official bodies serve to globalize profit-taking, globalize resource extraction, globalize poverty and concomitantly restrict what ought to be a global response. WTO forces those nations desiring a role in the world economy to abide by the lowest common denominator in both labor rights and environmental protection. If a government cracks down on a union and kills off those who try to organize collective bargaining, that is allowed by WTO. If a nation has lax environmental laws, that is called free trade. As a result of high-tech communications, rapid transport, and weapons proliferation, NAFTA and the WTO keep humanity under a yoke far broader than that of the biggest national empire ever forced together, bigger than the Roman Empire, bigger than even the British Empire. The ruling class on Planet Earth has succeeded, so far, in a bold new world order that guarantees vast wealth for an elite and massive poverty for much of the rest. The US military is the dragon guarding that palace, assisted by a few smaller draconics from other nations.

What is the result? On the one side, we just finished the bloodiest century in human history, with more than 100 million war deaths and more war refugees than any other period. On the other, directly related, we note that the richest 358 people on Earth have a combined personal income roughly equivalent to the poorest 45 percent of humanity—2.3 billion people. (United: 13)

Thus, when we recall the simultaneous beginnings of the rule of NAFTA and of the Zapatista rebellion in Chiapas, both on January 1, 1994, and when we see thousands of activists gathered in Seattle for a mass action in opposition to the World Trade Organization, we can perhaps put these concerns into context. The Zapatistas and WTO protesters are all demonstrating against the wastage of wealth on a few people of privilege while the mass of humanity suffers as a direct result. They are speaking out against the capital-intensive military expenditure that keeps the world's poor from simply taking the necessities they need, much as Jesus advised his hungry disciples to simply take a bit of food from the fields if they were hungry. Those fields are now guarded by US Marines and the poor of the world are raising a small but significant voice of protest.

It is also interesting to first note that peace researchers Kenneth Boulding and Bruce Russet assert that democracies don't go to war with each other, and to then examine the effects of WTO on democracy. For instance, after years of laboring and organizing, debating and weighing, citizen initiative and eventual legislative process, we at long last arrive at a piece of legislation designed to take many interests into consideration as it protects the environment. Then, WTO—using an unelected arbiter board meeting behind closed doors with minutes kept secret—simply waves it aside as restrictive of free trade. We can perhaps begin to appreciate the conflict.

It took years of wrangling to pass and defend the Endangered Species Act in the US. The intricacies of the scientific validity are still under close examination and reëvaluation. While the theories of species-area curve, applied to deforested areas, may turn out to be exaggerated in their predictive extinction estimates, so too are the economic forecasts of the effects of ESA on industry. (Libby: 184) This push-and-pull of research findings is ongoing and contributes to the wealth of data and conclusions at the ready in a freely examined question in a robustly democratic society. To paraphrase Winston Churchill, it's the worst process imaginable—except for all the rest.

When one global power is profoundly anti-democratic, as WTO is, the citizenry can be expected to resist with pressure toward more democracy.

When those who believe in nonviolence join them, we are less likely to witness bloodshed over justice struggles.

bang for the buck: where to make a difference

> *Poverty – not insufficient global food production – is the root cause of malnutrition....War and civil strife almost always cause upheaval in the food system and often result in widespread famine, as with the civil wars in Rwanda and Somalia.* (World: 16)

There are specific areas in which relatively modest shifts from military spending could produce major results. Since peace and humanitarian analysts have been making these points for decades, I will beg your pardon for my occasional lapse into the shrill call for change:

♥ 1-3 years of maternal education in 25 developing countries could reduce child mortality by up to 15 percent. (World: 15)

♥ Provision of vitamin A to children in developing nations could prevent much of the most severe manifestation of such deficiency, blindness. In fact, vitamin A deficiency is the single largest cause of childhood blindness of the quarter million children who go blind annually. (World: 17) What a tiny price to pay for the right to sight.

♥ In 1990 alone, 26 million people worldwide suffered brain damage to some degree from a simple shortage of iodine. (World: 17) This is totally preventable, obscenely inexpensive and literally stupid for us as the "wise ones," to allow.

♥ In developing nations, half the pregnant women—and their unborn inside them—suffer from anemia. (World: 17) This simple iron deficiency exists alongside the iron cross of militarism hung heavily around the neck of these poorest of the poor. For the cost of one Trident submarine we could fix this problem for decades.

♥ One in five humans lives without acceptable housing. (World: 17) What could the $20 billion paid by the US taxpayers waging war in the former Yugoslavia between 1992-1997 buy in habitat for humanity?

♥ One in four humans on Earth has no access to safe drinking water. (World: 17) What could the $10 billion we've spent killing Iraqis since 1991 have provided for our sisters and brothers around the world?

♥ Half of humanity has no access to adequate sanitation. (World: 17) Could we make a dent in that by unilaterally laying down our illegal, unusable and immoral nuclear weaponry that is currently costing us some $67.3 million each and every day?

consumption bomb: craters of imperial extraction

What the so-called "developed nations" remove from the so-called "developing nations" has been and remains the greatest theft of all time. From slavery to mining, from cheap labor to rainforest denudation, the list of the booty stolen from the people and the land is spectacular. Indeed, one may more appropriately term those poor countries "maldeveloped." It's all done with military might; without guns and bombs it would never have happened and it could not possibly continue.

Even the resources that do not go into military production can cause shooting war conflict. In 1988, after a long period of copper mining in Bougainville in Papua New Guinea, during which indigenous economies were destroyed by the environmental impacts of the mining, guerrillas began a war of secession. They were driven to secede by a devastating combination of deforestation, mine tailing pollution of available water, ruination of arable land and elimination of fish stocks. (Renner: 126)

In another wartorn nation, Liberia, the various factions plunder the natural resources to pay for their internal warfighting capabilities and for their leaderships' personal wealth. They go to lethal lengths to obtain those natural resources. Charles Taylor's National Patriotic Front of Liberia extracts rainforest timber, rubber and mineral resources. ULIMO-J and ULIMO-K, two other factions, battle each other and anyone else over diamonds and other mineral resources. (Miall: 131)

The rape of the Earth, the destruction of the environment, thus becomes a cause for war. Whether we are talking about Ferdinand and Isabella 500 years ago or President Doe of Liberia in our era, the leaders who make war are always looking for ways to finance that capability. The nonrenewable environment is rich in those cash conversion opportunities—at least in the historical short run. When we are willing to betray the future generations, it works well for a few hundred years.

And a militarized leadership usually sees no other way, since it sees no other path to power. As Ronald Reagan said when confronted in a budget meeting with his closest advisors, some of whom were cautioning against his $1.5 trillion budget-busting Pentagon build-up, "Defense is not a budget issue." Leadership often simply cannot understand any other options, even if they are wrecking the environment for the gain of ideological or "national security" ends rather than personal monetary gain. A mention of nonviolence is regarded as nubilous naiveté; it's not an option on the menu of the nation-states.

In the maldeveloped world, this model has transited from the raw colonial model through the imperialistic method and is very much alive in the way that the trade agreement bodies conspire to force the planet to continue this paradigm. The implications are profound, even where there are not currently shooting wars, because all activity is pointed toward extraction of natural and human resources for someone's profit, usually a rich corporation with its "local" suppliers. Those peripheral nation rulers are a relatively small-time rich class; they often own the extraction companies as well as the political process in the smaller nations and work directly with the transnationals in that systemic extraction.

Vandana Shiva notes that this not only changes the local subsistence economies for the worse, it changes the very culture of the countryside wherever it occurs, and it seems to be occurring everywhere. The extractive model favored by WTO, and GATT before it, promotes an increasing disintegration of the basic warp and woof of social fabric. It has "increasingly pushed women to work for the production of sustenance, while men have been drawn into military and profit-seeking activities." (Shiva: 1) The globalization of trade with no links to human rights is the greatest annihilator of indigenous cultures extant.

Clearly, then, a prime consumption question is the sheer expense of money and material on the arsenals of the world. While the direct ecological effects of the extraction of strategic materials were addressed in the first section, the consumption of money on war and war preparation itself can reduce the standard of living for many more than it helps, even as it fuels the predictions, expectations, fears and anticipation of war. The amount of money devoted to the militaries takes from the mouths of those who hunger, as Eisenhower warned in his farewell address decades ago, but it also creates a self-fulfilling prophesy of conflict management by the only tool we then possess, violence.

In the US, the defense and foreign aid budgets are the single largest source of government funding for private corporations. (Hartung, 8/99: 1) This gravy train has been given various rationales, but the greatest all-purpose justification from 1945-1991 was the Cold War. The West's goal of stopping and reversing the trend toward worldwide communist revolution and domination is accomplished. That threat is gone, evaporated. The smoke is now cleared and we see that the military machinery clanks along with no clear reason other than profit and perpetuation.

Who pays? If you have a job in the US, you do. From your income tax withholding comes a half-trillion annually—about half of the discretionary spending allotted to Congress. You pay for the US arsenal and you pay for the arsenals around the world. More than half of US weapons sales are now being financed by taxpayers right here, not by the overseas nation-states who receive these sophisticated weapons systems. (Hartung, 8/99: 1)

The Pentagon itself promotes US-made weapons to foreign buyers, many of them despots in their own countries. US troops perform weapons displays for them in the field, paradropping from screaming warjets or firing super-accurate missiles at airborne or ground targets. Some of these soldiers, these participants and witnesses, will describe for us this free service to the war industries, this product demonstration, conducted by the armed forces and never billed to the advertising budgets of the private corporations who await the purchase orders for the guns, electronics, jets or boats. (Hanson) In fiscal year 1996, for example, the US government spent $7.9 billion to promote these deadly products to foreign governments. (Hartung, 8/99: 1) Thus, the workers pay not only for the bristling biggest military in the world, but for the corporate welfare items that pad out the obscenely high executive salaries and bonus packages of the officers of Raytheon, General Electric and the myriad war profiteers. This concentration of weaponry and wealth is inherently unjust and therefore a driver to conflict; further, it enforces disparities by providing the threats necessary to oppress those who might try to gain their fair share.

What are these "opportunity cost" trade-offs? For the cost of just two Tomahawk cruise missiles we could double the conflict prevention budget for the 55-member Organization for Security and Cooperation in Europe. (Hartung, 4/99: 1) With a seriously beefed-up budget for nonviolent methods of conflict management, perhaps OSCE could have reduced the level of violence in Kosovo in the spring of 1999, obviating the excuse for war. It is becoming impossible to ignore these connections.

sources

Barash, David, ***Approaches to Peace: A Reader in Peace Studies***. New York: Oxford University Press, 2000.

Center for Defense Information, ***1997 CDI Military Almanac***. Washington DC: CDI, 1997.

Hanson, Barry, lecture, 22 September 1999.

Hartung, William D., "The Costs of NATO Expansion Revisited," NYC: World Policy Institute, 21 April 1999.

Hartung, William D., "Corporate Welfare for Weapons Makers: The Hidden Costs of Spending on Defense and Foreign Aid," Washington DC: CATO Institute, #350, 12 August 1999.

Homer-Dixon, Thomas F. and Jessica Blitt, editors, ***Ecoviolence: Links Among Environment, Population, and Security***. Lanham MD: Rowman & Littlefield Publishers, 1998.

Libby, Ronald T., ***Eco-Wars: Political Campaigns and Social Movements***. NYC: Columbia University Press, 1998.

Miall, Hugh, et al., ***Contemporary Conflict Resolution: The Prevention, Management and Transformation of Deadly Conflicts***. Cambridge UK: Polity Press, 1999.

Renner, Michael, "Transforming Security," in: Worldwatch Institute, ***State of the World 1997***. New York: W.W. Norton & Company Ltd., 1997: 115-131.

Shiva, Vandana, ***Close to Home: Women Reconnect Ecology, Health and Development Worldwide***. Philadelphia: New Society Publishers, 1994.

Sivard, Ruth Leger, ***World Military and Social Expenditures 1996***. Washington DC: World Priorities, 1996.

United Nations Development Programme, ***Human Development Report 1996***. New York: Oxford University Press, Inc., 1996.

Westing, Arthur H., editor, ***Cultural Norms, War and the Environment***. NYC: Oxford University Press, 1988.

World Resources Institute, ***World Resources: 1998-1999***. New York: World Resources Institute, 1998.

Energy for war: fueling conflict <u>and</u> the arsenals

The Gospel assures us that the way of the Lord involves great sacrifice, separation from family and community, persecution, jail, even death. Today, thousands of people wait in the desert of Saudi Arabia, willing to make these same sacrifices for the false gods of "oil" and "lifestyle." They are there because war is part of the "the American way of life."
—Moana Cole, Susan Frankel, Ciaron O'Reilly, Bill Streit, the "ANZUS Plowshares Community," written before publicly hammering on war planes in a "Use of Deadly Force is authorized" zone on Griffiss Air Force base, January 1, 1991, in nonviolent resistance to the overwhelming preparations for war in the Gulf. (O'Reilly: 2)

Sonnet to Nonviolence

As hearts the hope for peace and love embrace
Specters of death encroach on foreign soil
Engorge themselves up the god of oil
Pluck hope of peace from depths of outer space
Mete punishment for color, creed and race.
From sinful legacy of death recoil
Compassionate for those our wars despoil
Absorb the pain; God turns away Her face.
Respect for life, a gift that's sweetly fair
The clouds of war are mocking that belief.
What fetid evils bring earth soon to grief.
Resistance lights the way of those who dare.
Empowerment of love that shines within
In gentleness will let new life begin.

—Georgeen D'Haillecourt (D'Haillecourt: 10)

The world—some select portions of it—is rich in oil. It is our capital, our savings, that we have inherited from the entire Cambrian time on planet Earth. No one spent any of it for hundreds of millions of years. Nature simply made deposits in the account.

Suddenly, with the invention of the internal combustion engine, we are drawing on the savings and we see the numbers are huge so we live it up. Humanity has been on an oil spending spree—or, our oil machinery has been on a bender—since the beginning of the 20th century and the end is in sight. We have squandered an enormous gift and polluted the skies, waters, soils and tissues of every being on the globe with the effluents and aerosolized after-products of this bounty. The Consumption Age—relying upon the Carboniferous Age—is literally burning holes in our environment and the remaining reserves are a part of that very environment. We have a cause for war and an effect of war, all inherent in the use of fossil fuels.

In a positive ("positive" in the sense that an AIDS test can be "positive" or a family history for heart failure can be "positive") feedback loop of massive negativity and tragic irony, the militaries of the "First World" consume so much nonrenewable energy and such a high percentage of the world's valuable and rare strategic minerals that they themselves are a major driver in the militarized quest for more, more, more. Whoever gets more of a limited, nonrenewable resource must do so by force of arms, thus the mutually reinforcing dynamic.

Worldwatch Institute reports, for example, that the militaries of the world consume about as much energy as the entire economy of Japan—approximately six percent of the global annual energy budget. "A US-made F-16 fighter warplane burns more fuel in an hour than the average US car does in one year. Militaries account for nine percent of the iron and steel consumed each year." (Miller: 16)

"Resource depletion," writes David Malin Roodman, analyst for the Worldwatch Institute, "like pollution, also carries a hidden cost: that of depriving future generations of access to limited natural resources, such as oil and old-growth timber." (Roodman: 173) So the "protection" afforded by the Pentagon, the single largest user of fossil fuel products on the planet, is more a theft than a savings. The millions of gallons of jet fuel burned by warjets patrolling the Middle East, dropping the occasional bomb on Iraq, is not protecting oil, the interest of the future generations or even the security of the US in the moment; bombs cannot protect oil any more than bullets can stop rising seas due to the greenhouse effect. Indeed, when we add the fiscal and ecological expense of a military machine to the costs of fossil-fuel burning-caused global climate change, the downside of conflict management by use of military hardware becomes overwhelming.

During war over oil, in a new profundity of irony, the oil consumed was staggering. Just one division of armored tanks burned more than 600,000 gallons of fuel per day; each F-15 in afterburner gulps down 240 gallons per minute; four entire aircraft carrier groups "had" to throttle their way across the planet's oceans to assemble in the Persian Gulf in order to wage war to protect their ability to throttle their way around the Earth. Just *one* of these carriers—not counting its retinue of smaller war ships—the *USS Independence*, turned two million gallons of carbon-based fossil fuel into heat and airborne waste. The estimate of the 46-day war total oil consumption by the US-led UN forces to protect cheap oil: more than 900 million gallons. (Thomas: 127)

Thus, our paradigmatic decisions—what kind of car do I drive and what kind of conflict management do I subscribe to?—will change the world. It all matters, deeply. Our very lifestyle choices—what kind of transport we choose, how we heat our homes or power our lights, whether we buy locally-grown lumber and produce or purchase that shipped from thousands of miles away—all those choices affect the chances of war over resources. When an oil company came to my rural county in northern Wisconsin, wanting to drill, I was asked to be on a Wisconsin Public Radio talk show to present the opposing viewpoint. As this happened in 1992, the year after the Gulf War, the first thing I did was to thank the invading oil company for helping me to make my car-buying decision to purchase America's best mileage subcompact at the time. "I want to help save the environment right now and I want to lessen the chances of war over oil in the future. The combination of the recent Gulf War over oil and the folks from the Amoco spin-off exploration company have made up my mind for me," I said.

In fact, for most Americans, the vehicle they chose to drive is the single largest energy and environmental decision they will make. Add to that—and clearly linked to that—this decision is one of the most important they will make about affecting the chances for war in the future. If we vote for peace candidates and then pay for war by purchasing inordinate amounts of energy or fossil-fuel-intensive goods, we negate our own philosophies and actions. We pay cheaper prices than government-subsidized industries can offer, but, as Germany's Wuppertal Institute president, Ernst von Weizsacker said, "prices do not tell the ecological truth." This was borne out in recent studies that show the costs of driving in the US—health, pollution, time wasted in traffic, the DoD in the Mideast, accidents—total \$300-350 billion annually. To pay for it all at the pump, where it must be paid for to remove the government subsidy from gasoline-powered cars, we would have to pay an additional \$2.60 per gallon, roughly tripling the current price. (Roodman: 173) This subsidy is paid for in part by taxpayers, in part by insurance premiums, and largely ignored and put into the pile of unpaid bills that absolutely will be collected from children born and unborn. Once again, we find the hidden costs of conflict heaped on the shoulders of the average working person and her descendants.

sources

D'Haillecourt, Georgeen, ***Sirius Sonnets***. St. Louis MI: self-published, 1992.

Miller, John M., "War is a crime against the environment," *Peace News*, September-November 1999: 16+

O'Reilly, Ciaron, ***Bomber Grounded, Runway Closed: Prison Letters and Court Notes of a Gulf War Resister***. Marion SD: Rose Hill Books, 1994.

Roodman, David Malin, "Harnessing the Market for the Environment," in: Worldwatch Institute, ***State of the World 1996***. New York: W.W. Norton & Company Ltd., 1997: 168-188.

Thomas, William, ***Scorched Earth: The Military's Assault on the Environment***. Gabriola Island, Vancouver, British Columbia: New Society Press, 1995.

Section 4: Ecology of Peace

It does not do you good to leave a dragon out of your calculations, if you live near him.
—J.R.R. Tolkien

'And wear thou this': She solemn said,
And bound the holly round my head:
The polish'd leaves and berries red
  Did rustling play;
And, like a passing thought, she fled
  In light away.
—Robert Burns, "The Vision"

What would an ecology of peace look like? It would have to be diverse enough to value all of life and each human culture within the life of our species. It would have to be stable enough to withstand the strains of periodic shortage and suffering. An ecology of peace would need many and varied elements of immunological response to occasional outbreaks of jingoism, xenophobia, manipulative genius and even to emergent virulent violence.

We understand from the first two sections of this book—and from simply paying attention to life as we look back across the millennial divide—what the ecology of war looks like. We see what the ecology of peace is not. "Conflicts typical of the contemporary world cannot be resolved at gunpoint. They require not a recalibration of military tools and strategies, but a commitment to far-reaching demilitarization. Indeed, the military now absorbs substantial resources that could help reduce the potential for violent conflict if invested in health care, housing, education, poverty eradication, and environmental protection." (Renner: 116)

A crucial, too-often-overlooked, element of building an immunological response to violence and the despair attending it is the relief of laughter, the appreciation of the absurd. Thus, we can read Kurt Vonnegut about the carpet-bombing of Dresden on 13-14 February 1945 and find the wonder and touching humanity amidst the horror of roasted humanity. Nobel Peace Laureate Aung San Suu Kyi credits the ability of her people first to recognize and then to roar with laughter not only at the surrealism of imprisonment but even at torture by fellow Burmese so out of touch with reality they ask unanswerable questions and, when their prisoners cannot respond, hurt them further. "There are jokes about forced labor, about prison," says Daw Suu. "This is very much part of our Burmese culture." (Kyi: 156)

Indeed, Vàclav Havel noted that, if he would have been forced to increase his level of despair commensurate to the misery of Soviet bloc imprisonment, difficulties and monumental problems that faced him through his years of prison and political struggle against the Soviet empire, he would have quickly become petrified, his own statue. This metaphor was echoed by Martin Luther King Jr.'s warning about the "paralysis of analysis," not unlike substituting academic study for action. Just as lopsided and out of eco-balance is action without study and preparation.

King regarded the practice of prayer similarly, taking those who believe in it to the arena of social action, which is the heart of the inner mechanism of keeping an ecology of peace on track. "As a minister," he said, "I take prayer too seriously to use it as an excuse for avoiding work and responsibility." (Harding: 18)

In short, an ecology of peace involves the physical, the political, the economic, the cultural, the spiritual and the emotional/psychological. It is a diverse, challenging, self-correcting nonviolent process, achieving homeostasis by small adjustments, peaceful course alterations to meet any condition that threatens balance. The hard scientists and those who explore humanities alike are needed in this collective effort; neither category of expertise reigns in the overall picture of this ecology of peace; together they own a much larger piece of the solution.

sources

Harding, Vincent, ***Martin Luther King: The Inconvenient Hero***. Maryknoll NY: Orbis Books, 1996.

Kyi, Aung San Suu, ***The Voice of Hope: Conversations with Alan Clements***. NYC: Seven Stories Press, 1997.

Renner, Michael, "Transforming Security," in: Worldwatch Institute, ***State of the World 1997***. New York: W.W. Norton & Company Ltd., 1997: 115-131.

International law: citizens vs. kakistocracy

Sanctions are best considered as instruments of coercive diplomacy to persuade decisionmakers in the targeted state to reassess the costs and benefits associated with policies that have attracted the ire of the international community.

—David Cortright and George A. Lopez, International Peace Academy (Cortright: 223)

Government is a bad word nowadays and politics is worse. Politicians are so defiled and nepotistic that we can recycle this from 1987 (only the middle initials would be changed to update): *"No Democrats will be left in the race by the time we reach primary and caucus season. George Bush will run unopposed in November and lose."* (Taylor: 3) Citizens look for ways to fight back and some turn to the law. No law is formed in a vacuum. International law is no exception; if a law is made, someone is breaking it before it exists. Some nation-states have suffered what the Greeks called kakistocracy—government by the worst of men. International law can, in theory if not always in practice, keep these kakistocracies from damaging too much.

Our great challenge is to compel the leaders of the world into adopting a consistent approach to behaving legally or face the consequences. Those leaders seem unafraid to use the logic of the spouse-beater—"She made me do it"—and seem to get away with it. When, for example, the US led NATO to bomb Serbia and Kosovo in March, April, and May of 1999, we were frequently treated to pronouncements that Milošević forced us to bomb Belgrade. Saddam could have used the same logic when accused of environmental infractions, since he promised to fire his oil wells if attacked. He could have told the international community, "Bush forced me to keep my word; it is his fault." That is the logic of the average criminal and that is one reason we need international law.

There are several types of international law, including that mandated by: treaty between two or more nations; enough signing and ratifying nations to make it globally binding law; or custom. So, for example, a treaty between Russia and the US regarding nuclear weapons only applies to the two countries, whereas the Chemical Weapons Convention is the law for the entire world. (Renner: 160) The four distinct kinds of international law are generally referred to as: classical writings widely accepted; customary; treaties; and rulings of international courts. (Barash: 107)

Dating from the writings of 16th century Spanish legal scholar Francisco de Victoria, whose thesis was that war could be illegal if fought simply over religion or glory, and coming down to the revolutionary citizen-based process that led to the landmine ban, jurists and citizens alike have been laboring in the vineyards of legal proscription on certain practices for almost half a millennium.

The most widely known and accepted classical writing on the subject of war *vis-a-vis* the law is that of Hugo Grotius, the germinal 17th century Dutch jurist, who first effected a bridge between the religious doctrines dating to Augustine and Aquinas and the incipient field of international law. In "*On the Law of War and Peace,*" (1625), he borrowed Aristotle's term "natural law," claiming a cosmological law of right and wrong, permissible and impermissible, even if currently opaque or inscrutable to human-made lawgivers. The courts and scholars have been struggling to unmask, unpack and apply that natural law ever since.

And how may we enforce international law? There are two essential nonviolent methods: diplomatic censure consequence and smart sanctions.

In the field of conflict resolution the concept of "face" is key, and that is one of the best tools for enforcement of international law. Basically, a nation violating a standard of behavior ought to experience opprobrium—lose face through censure and reprobative embarrassment—a serious diplomatic consequence. This needs to be the case for violations of human rights, environmental and conduct in war situations alike. "*Once branded a treaty-breaker, a state may not be able to establish useful, reliable relationships with other states.*" (Barash: 108) This is a powerful deterrent and corrective, though far from infallible.

Nothing, in fact, is infallible, least of all guns, missiles and Kissingerian threats to, in effect, "do our bidding or we bomb." The truth of this is part of the point of international law, conflict resolution and nonviolence alike. The decisions about what methods of conflict management to use will either involve a more complete cost-benefit analysis (including the eco-costs and the likelihood of failure to prevail with armed force) or will fail to evolve, fail to become evermore adaptive for humanity.

Even as humanity demands that violent conflict become more like surgery and less like cremation, we also come to international law and sanctions with the intention of transforming them from the blunt instruments often serving the war system into precision tools for peacemaking—what Cortright and Lopez call "smart sanctions."

Sanctions are usually tied to UN Security Council resolutions, a process that accelerated exponentially when the Cold War ended. During the 1945-1990 period, the UNSC passed 647 resolutions—about one per month; during the 1990s, they passed 620 resolutions, more than one each week. (Cortright: 1) This is a tool that has been a part of the nonviolent toolkit for a long time; the bus boycott in Montgomery, Alabama in 1955 kicked off the modern US Civil Rights movement. It has been used successfully, most notably against apartheid in South Africa. But when it is enforced by violence or the threat of violence—as has clearly been the case with the US unilateral enforcement of its take-off policies from UNSC Resolution 687 against Iraq—the potential for sanctions as a tool of war is distinct. When the war system sniffs out a chance to coöpt an otherwise peaceful method of conflict managment, the results are usually negative.

The UN Convention on the Law of the Sea (UNCLOS), a process that began in 1958 and came into force 16 November 1994, is an example of the interference by the military and profiteers into the formation and application of international law. The US was one of those nations first calling for such an document and yet, because fair standards were applied to the economic terms of deep seabed mineral exploitation, the US has refused to sign. (Center: 5) This deprives US citizens of the environmental protections afforded by that treaty, blocked by same US legislative body—the US Senate Committee on Foreign Relations—that has bottled up so much progressive international treaties. Once again, the US has cut itself away from the mass of humanity and has adopted a rogue position.

An ongoing tension is that, in the application of domestic law, the state claims and achieves hegemony over the citizen, but in the application of international law the states all claim absolute sovereignty, refusing to become a citizenry of nation-states in a world of cooperative governance. This internal pull and push makes international law a fluid field, open to evolution.

On 3 December 1997 the landmine ban was first signed. By March 1, 1999 it went into effect; enough nations had signed on to the treaty to make it a self-executing law. It was long overdue; at least 80 percent of the casualties associated with landmines have historically been civilians. (Renner: 156) These "protected populations" have been hurt and this law goes to protect the innocent from being collateral damage in the swath of human conflict destruction. The landmine ban was the first international law written, promoted and shepherded through by a consortium of non-governmental organizations, the uniqueness of which was part of the recognition awarded by giving those NGOs and their spokeswoman, Jody Williams, the Nobel Peace Prize that year. The International Campaign to Ban Landmines was "just" citizenry, activists, from dozens of nations, who brought about a treaty that now applies globally because it was signed and ratified by enough governments, one-by-one. Noting the success and the bottom-up nature of the process, Williams called the collective of citizenry from around the Earth who choose to organize this treaty, "the new superpower." She suggests that this new power can do much more.

⚖

Here in the US, we continue to suffer under the 1946 Connally Reservation, an amendment attached to our agreement to abide by international law as ruled upon by the then-new International Court of Justice. It is that legalistic loophole that collides with the punishing international opprobrium faced by the US when, for example, it mines a harbor of a nation with which it is not formally at war—Nicaragua in this case—and the ICJ rules the US in violation of the law of nations. Ronald Reagan, the president who ordered that mining, declared our legal lack of obligation to follow ICJ rulings and then quietly ordered the mines removed, making the ruling *de facto* effective.

This is the closest we come to seeing international law "enforcement" mechanisms in action when applied to a major power. There is no global police force (contrary to US self-illusions). There is diplomatic consequence, and sometimes limited sanction. Some day, we may also see those who pollute our planet called to the bar of the International Criminal Court. "Pinochet the polluters" may one day become a credible deterrent (reference to Augusto Pinochet, Chilean former dictator who was held in Britain on house arrest in an attempt to extradite him to Spain for trial on charges of crimes against humanity committed by his military).

Those who favor the tool of economic sanction as used effectively against oppressors in some situations have been forced to sharpen their analysis in the light of the humanitarian crisis caused by sanctions against Iraq since 1990. Millions have perished and pollution has worsened as a consequence. One analyst noted, "We need smart sanctions, not smart bombs." From Kofi Annan to peace analysts David Cortright and George A. Lopez, the agreement is that comprehensive sanctions are generally destructive and targeted sanctions—e.g. arms embargoes and freezing assets—are vastly preferable. (Cortright: 223)

⚖

One of the most ambitious goals of those who wish to apply international law to increasing disarmament and decreasing violence is to first declare illegal and then to abolish all nuclear weapons. It has been illegal to wage nuclear war implicitly since even before the Manhattan Project was a gleam in General Grove's eye. Elements of international law that would have proscribed atomic weaponry are to be found as far back as the 1907 Hague Convention. Further items that, if read and understood in simple, black-and-white terms, would outlaw nuclear weapons are to be found in the 1925 Geneva Convention, the Kellogg-Briand Pact and the post-WWII Nuremberg Tribunal. Some elements go to environmental damage (Burroughs: 103), which, in the case of atomic weapons, is widespread and inherent in the mere production of this class of weapons, and has been tremendous with every explosion of every atomic or thermonuclear device. Some elements go to the protection of classes of people, especially noncombatants. Some pieces of international law proscribe offensive weapons, which is the nature of every nuclear weapon (they are either for counterforce first-strike use or retaliation against civilian centers, both of which are offensive). All these laws, signed by leaders and ratified by legislative bodies, apply legally to all states and all peoples. Since the early 1980s, citizens who engage in nonviolent civil resistance to nuclear weapons and their command and delivery components have been citing these international laws in various courts from Pennsylvania to then-West Germany, from Scotland to Australia. Success—hindered by the hegemony of national security—was rare.

Then, using precisely the same corpus of law used by civil resisters for more than 15 years, a group of 42 nations joined in a legal action asking the World Court to outlaw nuclear weaponry once and for all. It was the largest number of nations to ever bring a legal argument before the International Court of Justice and the trial of nuclear weapons took place during the last part of October 1995 and into November. The evidence was sifted, weighed and the justices deliberated and issued their ruling 8 July 1996: In virtually every conceivable circumstance, the mere possession of even a single nuclear weapon is illegal.

The World Court is composed of 15 judges or international law juriconsults chosen from a variety of legal systems worldwide and only exists to handle cases brought by nation-states or UN agencies. The two kinds of cases it hears are contentious, between nation-states, and advisory opinion. (Dewes: 6)

Illustrative of the involvement of the peoples of the world in this case, this long attempt to outlaw nuclear weaponry, is the example of the people and nation of Aotearoa/New Zealand. This small island nation of 3.5 million (in 1999) Maori and Euros, located off by itself in the South Pacific, was long opposed to the blatant imperious racism of the nuclear arms build-up by the US and other nations who left their own shores to seek someone else's part of the world in which to test their poisonous bombs. Virtually the entire South Pacific was in revolt against nuclear power hegemony. "Between 1945 and 1995, the United States (US), United Kingdom (UK) and France tested 317 nuclear weapons in Pacific Island States and Australia. In 1973, responding to growing public concern about the health and environmental effects, A/NZ and Australia asked the World Court to challenge the legality of France's atmospheric tests at Moruroa. During the following decade Belau (1979), Vanuatu (1982), the Solomon Islands (1983) and Aotearoa/New Zealand (1984) prohibited nuclear weapons from their territories, and in 1985 the region became the South Pacific Nuclear Free Zone." (Dewes: 7)

It was this movement that led the citizens of New Zealand to initiate the World Court Project in 1986 which sought to establish the illegality of nuclear weapons altogether. The World Health Organization joined the effort in 1993, asking the International Court of Justice to rule nuclear weapons an illegal risk to public health. The rich antinuclear history of New Zealanders truly began days after the bombing of Hiroshima and Nagasaki with a lecture against the bomb by philosopher Karl Popper in Christchurch, New Zealand, and continued more or less steadily through successive A/NZ administrations. The citizens began voicing their mass opposition to nuclear weapons early and have continued ever since, even preferring ultimately to resign from the 1951 security agreement ANZUS when, following New Zealand's refusal to berth nuclear weapons-bearing ships, the US said, essentially, "You accept nukes or you're out."

Generally speaking, antinuclear sentiment is globally majoritarian. From the 650 million signatures on the 1950 Stockholm Peace Appeal to the hundreds of nongovernmental organizations working on the Abolition 2000 campaign, the people of planet Earth, in the main, have not agreed with the nuclear weapons states. This has even applied to millions of the citizens of those very states, and one of the stated reasons that the ICJ agreed to hear the case in 1995 was the sheer number of signatures petitioning the governments of the world to ban these horrific weapons. The 1996 opinion has been construed by many as an invitation to challenge components of the global nuclear arsenals in the lower courts around the world; when judges hearing cases against nonviolent nuclear resisters have allowed such testimony, juries have generally responded favorably, even acquitting citizens of sabotage when they personally dismantle a small portion of a nuclear arsenal. This is a crucial link between the people, the opinion of each of us, and the highest human-written law on Earth, a tie which ought to empower citizens to keep on fighting for better, clearer international law on all matters military and environmental.

sources

Barash, David, "International Law," in ***Approaches to Peace: A Reader in Peace Studies***, David Barash, ed., NYC: Oxford University Press, 2000.

Burroughs, John, ***The (Il)legality of Threat or Use of Nuclear Weapons: A Guide to the Historic Opinion of the International Court of Justice***. Munster, Germany: LIT, 1997

Center for Defense Information, "The Law of the Sea," *Defense Monitor*, May 2000: 5+.

Cortright, David and George A. Lopez, ***The Sanctions Decade: Assessing UN Strategies in the 1990s***. Boulder CO: Lynne Rienner Publishers, 2000.

Dewes, Kate and Robert Green, ***Aotearoa/New Zealand at the World Court***. Christchurch, New Zealand: Raven Press, 1999.

Dycus, Stephen, ***National Defense and the Environment***. Hanover NH: University Press of New England, 1996.

Renner, Michael, "Budgeting for Disarmament," in: Worldwatch Institute, ***State of the World 1995***. New York: W.W. Norton & Company Ltd., 1995: 150-169.

Taylor, Paul, ***See How They Run: Electing the President in an Age of Mediaocracy***. NYC: Alfred A. Knopf, 1990.

Nonviolence: a new security

Nonviolence is the best form that man has worked out for peaceful change…I want to look upon nonviolence not only as a way to achieve our objectives, but also as a way of life…our structures – politics, economic, social and cultural, scientific and ideological, even defense and security – all of our structures must be reorganized.

—Dr. Kenneth Kaunda, founder and first president of Zambia, founder of the Kaunda Institute for Peace and Democracy (Sutherland: 107)

We are ready to undertake a peaceful political struggle with the communists, if only the destruction of the war can be stopped.

—Thich Nhat Hanh, plea to US to pull out of Vietnam, 1966 (Hanh: 57)

Theodore Rozak noted that a people, a nation, will use violence for a long time—a year, ten years, decades, literally hundreds of years—in order to struggle for liberation or for a return to their land. Then they try nonviolence for a week, it doesn't "work," and they revert to their violent ways, claiming that nonviolence is a naive, useless tactic. We can look to Northern Ireland, Southeast Asia, the Mideast and many familiar hot spots around our globe for such evidence.

But every once in a while, a person or a group of people convince their community to think more deeply about this, to go beneath and beyond the surficial instant test, the quickie gratification of shooting at some soldier of the empire. Occasionally, a serious struggle will commit to nonviolence, and when it does, it is generally on the path to eventual victory unless cynically derailed by overwhelming violence, as in the case of NATO's "humanitarian" bombing of Serbia and Kosovo for 78 days in the spring of 1999. That bombing destroyed the nonviolent work of nine years by the Kosovar Albanians, by empowering the "alternative," the Kosovo Liberation Army. The KLA, shielded by a massive rain of death from the sky, began to slaughter the oppressors, the Serb police and army. The people began to associate the KLA with liberation long sought, thus ruining the nonviolent revolution that had been ongoing and progressing for almost a decade.

A similar course of events—a nonviolent conflict destroyed by violence—took place in Russia in 1905, when generally nonviolent actions by the peasants and workers nearly toppled the Tsar and did force some democratic reform. When the resistance was taken over the Bolsheviks and Menshiviks in late 1905, however, and they initiated a campaign of armed uprising, the Tsar's troops grew fearful, defensive, and brutally violent, crushing the insurgency. (Sharp: 78) Thus, the increased "radicalness"—which was really a retreat into tired old violent tactics—ended democratic reform in Russia, one might say, until the first glimmer under Khruschev and finally the floodlight of Gorbachev's *glasnost* followed by *peristroika*, a restructuring that included partial disarmament and an abandonment—if not renunciation of—the paranoid yet expansionist Brezhnev Doctrine.

But given a chance, nonviolence works apparent miracles.

So it went in the Philippines, a land of great injustice and suffering under a US-installed dictator for more than three decades. There, after decades of guerrilla warfare throughout the outlying islands, the nuns and other community leaders began to prepare the populace for peaceful liberation. They talked and trained for ten years and the chance eventually came in 1986. When the revolt threatened to turn from a clear choice for democracy to a battle between two factions of the military, the organizers spread the word by mouth, by handbill, by radio. "It's time. Come into the streets."

And they did. The people filled the EDSA, the main, multilaned thoroughfare in Manila, blocking the tanks of rebellious faction, which were rumbling toward the tanks and troops prepared to defend the dictatorial Marcos faction. For days, the people spread love and flowers where there had been arrests and torture and martial law—so much for the notion that nonviolence only works against a "civilized" oppressor. They were Out There by the thousands and they succeeded; the Philippines won its democratic revolution nonviolently, with almost no casualties. It begs the counterfactual; what if the people had picked up the gun in downtown Manila and fought Marcos violently? The results may have been very different—and we may note the same for the Velvet Revolution in Eastern and Central Europe as well as the break-up of the Soviet Union into autonomous republics—due to the psychology of nonviolence. It is absolutely certain that there would have been many more casualties.

While most are generally aware of the big nonviolent victories, fewer are aware of the Filipina nuns, the Polish priests and the other "invisible" trainers who help the populace prepare to confront violence with nonviolence. It is an ongoing process nowadays, worldwide. The War Resisters

League and others are quietly training more of the young activists who oppose the greedy globalization forces of the WTO. Mubarak Awad and others brought sufficient nonviolence to the intifada to change its face. Even in the Himalayan foothills, organizers bring Gandhian nonviolence to illiterate villagers.

> *To my mind the most important factor in bringing about change in society is fearless thinking among the people, and Gandhi's contribution to the world was his generation of this power of fearlessness, particularly in the hearts of the downtrodden and poor. Thereafter they were about to stand up and say, "We won't tolerate this injustice." This fearlessness is a basic factor in bringing about long-lasting social change.*
>
> *The exploited and weak people and classes are so because they have lost the courage to stand up against injustice and exploitation. After a while, a sense of fatalism becomes fixed in the minds of these people, and they lose any confidence they once had in themselves. When this happens, people cannot even understand or recognize the nature of the injustice or exploitation to which the are subjected.*
>
> – Radha Bhatt, Lakshmi Ashram (Bhatt: 168)

I once approached a psychology professor about the possibility of him coming into my Theory and Practice of Nonviolence class to describe the psychology of nonviolence. He looked at me quizzically and queried, "What does psychology have to do with nonviolence?"

Truly, there is little else *but* the psychological or emotional "weapons" available to nonviolent practitioners.

There is also a clear psychology of violence, even when it is used sparingly, as in the intifada, or in many of the ethnic struggles for freedom. There are several elements in this study of motive, action and effect. Some basic principles of what happens when we use violence:

- Resentment, fear, hatred and reactionary violence are swift and virtually inevitable.
- Negotiations are immediately strained and may break off altogether.
- The violence is usually directed against the first available justifiable target, i.e., the women and children who do not so easily melt back into the urban or jungle or mountain landscape.
- Military forces may move into the area in greater numbers for longer periods of time.
- Paramilitaries are provided with more arms and evermore shrill

rhetoric, terrorizing with the tacit support of the official army.

💣 It is easy to fabricate incidents, e.g., a soldier is shot and the perps vanish but it is sworn to the media that they are the violent revolutionaries. This is a favorite tactic of the old military regime in Guatemala, using a new Mayan boy, just conscripted, as the sacrificial soldier. (Miron) Once a liberation movement stoops to violence, the oppressor can lie about them with impunity, bolstering their self-justification and casting doubt about culpability, even for major massacres.

💣 Human rights workers of all stripes—union leaders, political leaders, lawyers, village doctors—are in especial danger instantly and over the long term.

💣 Villagers are seen as a direct threat and their independence is assaulted by crop burning, forced conscription of the young men, etc., all methods to punish them for and to mitigate their support for the "g" (guerrillas).

💣 Foreign military aid generally increases to "preserve law and order," especially when trade and thus profits are threatened. The guerrillas are great for arms sales.

A particularly tragic example of these responses to violence happened to the nonviolent human rights leadership of the Ogoni people in Nigeria's delta region, which is oil country and heavily exploited by both foreign multinationals and the military elite. Indigenous peoples there suffered—and are still victimized—under triple oppressions of losing their traditional economy and lifestyle to the ecological devastation of unchecked oil extraction and processing, suppression of labor rights and the ability to bargain for living wages, and, finally, the increasing health effects of oil industry pollution. (Renner: 127) It is one of the salient examples of the dubious benefits of living where "liquid gold," is beneath tribal land.

The Ogoni responded in a mixed fashion, using both violence and nonviolence, and the reactions were thus also mixed. Ken Saro-Wiwa, a nonviolent human rights activist and writer, led a nonviolent campaign of resistance to the military and environmental offenses. He was beginning to get international attention and renown for his struggle. Then, an Ogoni chief lost control and attacked another tribal chief who supported the military government. Horrifically, the Ogoni chief threw the other into a fire to burn to death. The military went on a rampage, arresting the nonviolent leadership and attacking Ogoni villages, killing an estimated 2,000 and uprooting 80,000. (Renner: 127) All the international pressure couldn't save Ken Saro-Wiwa and eight other nonviolent Ogoni leaders, who were publicly executed by hanging as a direct result of violent resistance—even though it wasn't theirs. But that international clamor, which increased when the martyrs were murdered, did help to bring down the military government, demonstrating that the combination of violent and nonviolent resistance did have varying effects.

The Zapatistas of Chiapas, Mexico, present another example of mixing violence and nonviolence in an indigenous struggle; that effort has yielded mixed results in proportion to each method used. Though the beginning of the indigenous battle for environmental sustainability and human rights was announced by masked, armed revolutionaries on January 1, 1994, those Zapatistas have not been violent in deed. This confusion added to the uncertainties of their stance and rhetoric have led to a commensurately erratic governmental response. The worst manifestation of that reaction was the massacre of 45 nonviolent villagers in Acteal, accompanied by the heavy commitment of Mexican troops to the region. Thus, while the violent posture of the Zapatistas no doubt contributed to—or perhaps directly inspired—the brutal attack on Acteal—the general nonviolent behavior by those in rebellion has attenuated the possible violence by the Mexican troops. In addition, Christian Peacemaking Teams and others have streamed to the region to engage in explicitly nonviolent accompaniment, which has almost certainly helped to mitigate military response, since CPT and other groups of internationals are there to witness. The Acteal massacre resulted in swift and general opprobrium, to which virtually all governments are sensitive, especially those dependent on larger trading partners and aid suppliers whose citizenry may be touched by grassroots groups' outreach efforts.

It is axiomatic that populations engaging in nonviolent resistance are easier to sharply outline as "protected" under international treaty and customary law, giving a hook to those human rights groups who seek to cast the light of public scrutiny on indigenous struggles. Any resort by the oppressed to violence *removes* a media newspeg—contrary to the normal "if it bleeds it leads" journalistic dictum. When that bleeding is done on all sides, it's just another skirmish story among hundreds. When that bleeding is done by the pure-of-method, it becomes an attack by marauding troops on innocents and diplomatic consequences can be generated. That is a key—though too-often-missed—component of the power of nonviolence. When indigenous leadership abandons the Che Guevara romantic notions of revolutionary violence of the 1960s and enters the new wave of third millennium indigenous nonviolence they will advance much more quickly. When their supporters in rich countries realize the same, they will garner general public support for those indigenous populations much more easily.

where nonviolence is most challenged

One of the very hardest places to effect nonviolent victory is the little nation that is invaded and taken over by a huge nation. Thus, for example, a nonviolent victory in Tibet is much harder than, say, a democratic revolution in the Philippines. China is simply a monstrously large oppressor and sanctions against it have a pinprick effect. International disapproval is routine for the much more self-sufficient China than for the relatively tiny El Salvador, or Guatemala, or even the much larger Indonesia. How, then, will the Dalai Lama and his nonviolent troops ever liberate their homeland?

There are two keys that may work in the double lockdown of internal and external oppression.

First, unlike, for example, the ill-fated and unsupported nonviolent revolution of the Albanian Kosovars from 1990-1998, the outside global nonviolent movement must mobilize in support of Tibetan freedom, and they must do so on the terms set forth and directed by the Dalai Lama or whatever leadership is legitimate and has the allegiance of the nonviolent forces in Tibet. This global support must be serious and focused, willing to bring any nonviolent pressure to bear upon the Chinese government that the nonviolent indigenous forces propose. This includes organizing from external bases—within the home nations of the diverse nonviolent movement—and being prepared to interpose *en masse*, if invited.

Second, the forces within Tibet must remain strong and creatively nonviolent. Without their absolute nonviolence, leadership and organization, the liberation cannot happen.

Fortunately, the worldwide nonviolent movement may have learned its lesson about failing to adequately support indigenous nonviolent freedom movements. The KLA first began its violent popgun attacks on Serb police and Serb army forces in Kosovo in the late winter of 1998. This escalated Serb reprisals and set the stage for NATO intervention, already largely constructed by the 1995 Dayton fiasco, during which the US cut the Rugova government out of the deal. That shadow government, employing many of the most advanced techniques listed by Gene Sharp in his germinal studies on nonviolent struggle, appealed for international help but very few responded. The Albanian Kosovars, who had even gone so far as to self-impose a three percent income tax to pay for their nonviolent parallel infrastructures, were left twisting by both the US government *and* by the international nonviolent community. The results were predictable. Milošević felt his hands bound to violence and unbound to react to the unsupported leadership of Ibrahim Rugova. NATO stepped in to assume the international leadership vacuum and liberal doves sprouted talons in their support for the air attack of March-June, 1999. If the worldwide nonviolent movement didn't learn its lesson from that, it is without force, without much of a near-term future. "Nonviolence," asserts peace researcher Nigel Young, "has to be preemptive, not waiting for UN or state initiatives (like that of the US), and it must encourage the empowerment of the weak in such action." (Young: 206) To the extent that we understand and act on our responsibilities, we can in fact help Tibet and other little nations in similar straits.

Internally, the Tibetans continue to practice nonviolent resistance to a half-century of oppression. Sometimes it seems the monks and nuns—the moral and cultural leadership—are just getting warmed up. Their sense of inevitability of success, their willingness to hone Buddhist nonviolence to a fine edge, is truly inspiring. In accordance with the psychological principle that it is virtually impossible to simultaneously experience wrath and mirth, these local leaders employ creative humor to disarm their Chinese oppressors.

☺ In response to the reassertion of nonviolent resistance within Tibet, led by monks and nuns and beginning in September 1987, a group of monks at one monastery was ordered to write self-criticism. They folded the forms into paper airplanes and launched them at each other in a daring act of open nonviolent resistance. (Kramer: 5)

☺ When similarly confronted by Chinese authorities, another group of monks in a different monastery set about a debate, employing elegant Buddhist dialectics, "proving" that, actually, China was probably a part of Tibet. (Kramer: 5)

☺ In the face of martial law decree banning images of the Dalai Lama, street vendors placed photos of other Lamas in frames on tables for sale and displayed one empty picture frame in the midst of the rest, obviously representing the Dalai Lama. (Kramer: 5)

Importantly, the Tibetans are not only outreaching to international NGOs and nation-states that may be sympathetic, they are educating the Han Chinese, the Chinese abroad, Chinese intellectuals, Chinese students and the Chinese dissident/democracy movement. The Dalai Lama, in his inimitable disarming fashion, has noted publicly that "the Chinese are a great people. If you look at their accomplishments, you can only respect them...We must send them our compassion, for they too are suffering." (Kramer: 6)

There is another challenge to those who successfully engage in nonviolent revolution; a nation-state must be preserved against all threats. This exigency has invariably led the nonviolent revolutionary leadership—from India to Zambia to the Philippines to Czechoslovakia and elsewhere—to "pragmatically" cave into those who demand a military, or at the least, an armed police force.

This will present a serious question until the nation in question recognizes and accepts the principles of Civilian-Based Defense as a permanent part of the readiness and commitment of the entire populace. Until CBD is entrained into the education and culture of a people, they will be forced into choosing between certain violent defeat or violent defense.

Dr. Gene Sharp of the Albert Einstein Institution at Harvard proposed the CDB theories, which came out of his half-century of research into the power and methods of nonviolence. His assertion, based upon evidence from hundreds of documented cases, is that a people can become ungovernable and thus unconquerable in most cases, if they choose a seriously mass nonviolent approach. Sharp's methods, if carried to a maintenance stage, are the best hope for a nation that is intent upon maintaining their freedom nonviolently.

nonviolent defense of the Earth

Negotiation is the ultimate purpose of most nonviolent action; indeed, it is the goal, as well-noted by Dr. Martin Luther King, Jr., in his "Letter from a Birmingham Jail," written in the brutal campaign in that Alabama city in 1963. Thus, when someone frees dolphins from killing nets and faces jail time, when Native Americans sit on railroad tracks to stop shipments of chemicals across their reservation, or when people of East Liverpool, Ohio, hold nonviolent demonstrations in opposition to a toxic waste facility situated near an elementary school (Terkel: 8), the idea is to bring the authorities to their senses, to the bargaining table, and to a better agreement. Nonviolence is the best weapon we have to save the Earth and it is particularly sharply differentiated from the kind of power that pollutes with weaponry and disregard for the Earth, i.e., military power.

When people "cross the line" in opposition to the destruction committed by the use of violence, by the mere threat to kill, they are standing in complete contradiction to the methods used by the militaries of the world. Thus, the Shoshone, Mormons, Franciscans and others symbolically trespass at the Nevada test site and keep the pressure on the public and the politicians to change, to get more strict about no nuclear testing.

Indeed, the group Greenpeace was started over the issue of environmental effects of nuclear testing on Amchitka Island, Alaska. The little old boat *Greenpeace* sailed into the icy ocean waters, drawing the attention of the people of Alaska, Canada, the US and the world. The DoD relented and turned the island into a bird sanctuary. (Terkel: 16) Nonviolent action shines the light of public scrutiny on bad environmental practices even when the official lights have been turned out and put away.

When authorities decided to truck 7,223 loads of PCB-contaminated soil to a landfill in Warren County, Ohio, they were shocked by a campaign of nonviolent resistance, since the folk who lived around there were generally poor and black. "It's one thing to be poor," said one protester, "and it's another thing to be poor and poisoned." More than 500 were arrested in the campaign, mostly for lying down in the highway to block the trucks. (Terkel: 16)

The courage and intense training and organization that are always a potential in the nonviolent movements, coupled with good conflict resolution techniques, are the best bet to save our sweet home, Mother Earth. It is not enough to "study war no more." We have to get good at waging peace. When we do, we will see the damage fall away and the Earth begin to heal. It's magic, but here is the secret to the trick; it's lots of hard but inspired work, based entirely on love for life.

sources

Bhatt, Radha, "Lakshmi Ashram: a Gandhian perspective in the Himalayan Foothills," in ***Healing the Wounds: The Promise of Ecofeminism***, Judith Plant, editor, Philadelphia PA: New Society Publishers, 1989.

Hanh, Thich Nhat, ***Love in Action: Writings on Nonviolent Social Change***. Berkeley CA: Parallax Press, 1993.

Kramer, Katherine G. and Yeshua Mossier-Puangsuwan, "The Tibetan Nonviolent Struggle," *Frontline*, Spring 1999: 4-6.

Miron, Kurt, personal communication, July 1998.

Plant, Judith, editor, ***Healing the Wounds: The Promise of Ecofeminism***. Philadelphia PA: New Society Publishers, 1989.

Renner, Michael, "Transforming Security," in: Worldwatch Institute, ***State of the World 1997***. New York: W.W. Norton & Company Ltd., 1997: 115-131.

Sharp, Gene, ***The Politics of Nonviolent Action***. Boston: Porter Sargent Publishers, 1973.

Sutherland, Bill and Matt Meyer, ***Guns and Gandhi in Africa: Pan African Insights on Nonviolence, Armed Struggle and Liberation in Africa***. Trenton NJ: Africa World Press, Inc, 2000.

Terkel, Susan Neiburg, ***People Power: A Look at Nonviolent Action and Defense***. NYC: Lodestar, 1996.

Young, Nigel, "Peace Studies at the Millennium," in Larry Fisk & John Schellenberg, editors, ***Patterns of Conflict: Paths to Peace***, Peterborough, Ontario: Broadview Press, 2000.

Constructive conflict

> *If nonviolent action is boldly taken it does allow men to speak out their deepest feelings; and if it is boldly taken, it does allow them to feel that they are standing up to others like men....In this very process, one's hatred of the other can be forgotten, because it is beside the point; the point is to change one's life.*
>
> —Barbara Deming, "On Revolution and Equilibrium" (Deming: 185)

Where we wish to go dictates how we journey; if we wish to paddle our kayaks from the Apostle Islands of Lake Superior to the Sault Ste. Marie locks and eventually out through the Great Lakes Seaway we will pack differently than if we are going to sail from South Florida to John's Pass. We choose a different vessel and we take unrelated maps and charts. We dress in almost opposite fashion and almost speak another tongue.

This is how we come to conflict. If we have one tool in common, it is our nonviolent creativity; much of the time each battle will call for a seemingly strange set of implements. If we wish to preserve wilderness in the western US from bombing range expansion we may approach the problem in a way that emphasizes the commonality between Native Rights and local economic sustainability, eliciting the help of wilderness preservationists through national lobby groups. When we come to a toxic dump from weapons manufacturing on the East Coast, it may work better to enlist the national peace movement, the environmental justice groups, and local legislators. The sources of power are out there and the methods to tap them are within us.

How do we prove our case when advancing our interests in a clean environment and a peaceful planet? Environmental ethicist Kristen Shrader-Frechette reminds us that charismatic and emotional appeal is one way; scrupulous science is another. She calls the former soft ethics and the latter hard ethics. "Because the most serious environmental conflicts concern situations of factual and probabilistic uncertainty, following scientific norms of avoiding false positives, in a context of uncertainty, often encourages false negatives, failing to recognize environmental damage when it occurs. What such ethics gain because of their scientific credibility, they lose because of their generality. What they gain because of the epistemological conservatism, they lose because of their inadequate environmental protectionism." (Shrader-Frechette: 783)

She goes on to argue for a third way, beyond the heuristic inspiration of an Aldo Leopold (or, on the peace side, Helen Caldicott) or the inscrutably inconclusive lab-coated data-driven but credible scientific analysis of a Robert Henry Peters (Gene Sharp from the nonviolence field). Shrader-Frechette proposes "Sound environmental ethics, at least at present, require a 'practical ecology' based largely on case studies and rules of thumb." (Shrader-Frechette: 784)

Just so with our methods of conflict management. On the one hand, we are moved by the faith-based call to beat swords into plowshares and by the willingness of a handful of resisters to take the consequences of beginning that process themselves, perhaps going out to hammer on an A-10 Wart Hog that throws depleted uranium at the Balkans or Iraq. These brave resisters use simple right and wrong arguments; it is wrong to kill humans and pollute the Earth and it is right to stand in the way and to suffer the consequences. On the other hand, we have the Michigan Study on the Causes and Correlatives to War, which has been gathering data for decades and, as far as anyone knows, has not been able to apply a single solution to prevent a single shooting war, even though no one would find fault with their methodologies.

Key, perhaps, is the integration and the resolve to action, avoiding both the ignorance of voluntary stupidity and what Dr. King called the "paralysis of analysis." As always, in the promotion of conflict resolution and nonviolence alike, we promote a third way. We propose taking cloth bags into the grocery store so that, when the bagger asks, "paper or plastic," we can say, "neither, thank you, I have a different approach." When the utilities offer coal or nuclear we can mount photovoltaics or spin the wind. When we hear the State Department offer the president a choice of war or standing by idly to watch genocide, we can suggest nonviolent methods of intervention, interposition, persuasion, even coercion. There is almost always a third choice, or a fourth or a thousandth. Again, we are called to collect data, to muster our collective will, and to create something unique. Conflict transformation requires nothing less.

miracles and war prevention

The miracle may be conflict management, a field under development since the end of World War II and increasingly unbound internationally since the end of the Cold War. Theorists give two overall methods of prevention of shooting war, light and deep. An example of light would be the fire extinguisher of peace negotiations toward a ceasefire. An example of deep prevention is the fireproof construction of a just peace—and the perception of justice by all aggrieved parties. A just peace is an equitable sharing of natural resources and is much harder to achieve on an overall, systemic basis than is a temporary agreement to stop the killing. Once an equitable solution is finally achieved, however, it reduces innate likelihood of violence amongst natural stakeholders, heading off shooting conflict long before it degenerates to that point. (Miall: 97)

Peace researchers have asked some basic questions about war, causation, and antecedents. From elements of their answers, we can begin to identify possible preventive measures short of armed intervention or its threat. The scope of this book is not amenable to a complete look at this pantheon of war prevention tactics, but we can examine some in the context of the environment in general and fresh water in particular.

There are four necessary conditions to war:

- One, the willingness of humans to kill members of our own species.
- Two, the belief in society that resort to armed conflict is justified under some circumstances.
- Three, the absence of effective antiwar devices.
- Four, the existence and availability of weaponry. (Miall: 98)

Humans are capable of killing each other, obviously. However, they were also capable of slavery, cannibalism, belief in the divine right of kings and other noxious and now unacceptable practices. To change this value, this social more, will be a matter of long and deep prevention indeed. From the Just War doctrine to the vague UN laws on war to the popular culture portrayal of violence-for-good as heroic and patriotic, we are up against a deep prevention problem when we tackle the notion of nation-state permission to go to war. This will take effort through our religious and educational infrastructures and will take profound change.

Antiwar devices may be our best light prevention hope. While the UN peacekeeping forces have a checkered history of violence prevention, they are learning. And the incipient Peace Force—the latest reincarnation of Gandhi's original vision of an international Shanti Sena "disarmy"—is promising, but years from its first trials of nonviolent interposition or intervention.

The small arms trade alone has made sure that, since the invention of Mr. A. Kalashnikov's hellish little gun in the eponymous year of '47, the fourth condition necessary for war is satisfied for much of humanity. Sadly, this is a robust element in WTO and other "free trade" organizations and control mechanisms. While it is illegal to ship a bale of marijuana, it is fine to launch ships with holds full of AK-47s, cluster bombs, C4 plastic explosives and all the other weaponry designed and destined to cost the lives of unsuspecting villagers throughout the maldeveloped world. Though WTO forces nations to in turn force their indigenous farmers to buy seed instead of save it, the same global economic engine runs on arms transfers to both sides of most wars. Until normative work is done at the international level and that is translated into proscriptions on arms sales, we will see the world literally up in arms, ready to shed blood at the drop of a water sluice.

Good conflict managment doesn't oppose any economic system based on a distaste for competition. Syracuse University Social Conflict professor Louis Kriesberg reminds us to differentiate between contest and conflict: "Competition is continuous and impersonal. Conflict is intermittent and personal." (Kriesberg: 2) If it becomes personal, it is conflict, by definition in the field of Conflict Resolution. What Kriesberg leads us to is what Harvard conflict researchers Roger Fisher and William Ury have long held, that relationship is key. Separating the people from the problem is our initial task, in order, then, to preserve the relationship. (Fisher: 21) If we could internalize this piece of the theory and nothing else, we would advance in all our movements for both peace and environmental protection. We would put a human face on the other, which is the first step toward persuading polluters to clean up and warriors to a peace conversion. This does not mean we do not have an ultimatum, a "best alternative to a negotiated agreement" that may involve force, but we use nonviolent force and we do everything we can to avoid resorting to that least-creative option, everything we can to build relationship so it doesn't come to that. This is in direct opposition to the "radical" viewpoint that "we don't negotiate with *those* kind of people." Wrong. We negotiate *and* we use force when necessary to push those negotiations forward based on remediating power asymmetries.

Our next, and most major, step is to develop a method of communication that strives toward agreement on the search for fair standards. (Fisher: 81-94) This requires all our creativity and may involve extreme nonviolent methods in order to bring the opponent to the table, as Dr. King called for in his "Letter from Birmingham Jail," a classic document in the field of nonviolent theory, since he wrote it while incarcerated for standing up to seemingly invincible oppressive forces in the summer of 1963. King never advised the use of nonviolent resistance for its own sake or even for a purely moral witness, but rather as the only moral option under certain circumstances of long-suffering injustice, and then for the purposes of bringing sides together, not driving them apart.

Conflict was formerly regarded as a linear continuum of a few steps: a triggering event, a shooting match, and a negotiated solution. We now understand conflict as an intricate cycle with no real beginning or end.

Along the upward or downward spiral we find accumulated grievances, manifestation of conflict, escalation, deëscalation, agreement, post-accord peacebuilding, accumulated grievances, manifested conflict, and so on. The hope is not to eliminate conflict but rather to make the methods of management increasingly nonviolent and more just. It is not unlike engineers who work *with* the laws of physics in order to get something done rather than waiting for gravity and the Second Law of Thermodynamics to cause harm. Conflict is a fact of life; it is up to humans to manage it with intelligence and skill.

Kriesberg parses out the difference between destructive conflict and constructive conflict and gives the reasons for *desiring* conflict under select circumstances. Simply, constructive conflict uses nonviolent means toward just ends and seeks to improve both the conditions of the oppressed and the relationship between oppressed and oppressor until there is no more oppression, taking as many trips through the conflict cycle as it requires. (Kriesberg: 25) Prototypically, Gandhi's method of achieving independence for India from Britain was not "total freedom now," a demand that sounds as though it came from a Black Power rally of the late 1960s or perhaps a black ski-masked contingent at the Battle of Seattle. Gandhi won the freedom for India one "reformist" struggle after the next, each designed to not merely achieve a victory but to actually improve the relationship between all parties while doing so. Indeed, many of the foundational aspects of the theories of conflict management come straight from Gandhi, or from analysis of his approach. (Miall: 41)

There is no such thing as a simple, cookie-cutter method of intranational or international conflict management; the complexities are innumerable and will confound those who try the "learned-it-in-Somalia-let's-apply-it-to-Serbia" tactic, or the "learned-it-in-class-and-here-I-am-in-Columbia" recipe for disaster.

Some of the questions we ought to ask:

- What are the underlying interests of each conflictual party?
- Are any of the interests of one party or both simply unfair?
- What are the internal dynamics that may determine who has the power to actually negotiate for one side or another?
- Are there influential intermediaries from all sides who can engage in discrete, protracted talks with each other without being beholden to any particular leadership or constituency?
- Do the underlying interests seem to be the same, or complementary?
- What unstated conflict drivers exist (e.g. are there ancient revenge motives behind a water rights struggle, or are there "silent partners" who speak softly but carry big influence?)?

It is important to assess the situation objectively and as comprehensively as can be done; without a flinty-eyed look at a conflict from as many sides as possible, one cannot hope for an effective idea of how to analyze it, much less be of some possible assistance. The credibility of the third party is probably of greater import than the credibility of the conflictual parties, in the sense that some objective standards are expected, some rational analysis is required of any party hoping to influence a conflict away from violence and toward a negotiated outcome. Indeed, hyperbole and misrepresentation is expected from the conflictual parties, especially in the initial stages of negotiation while positional bargaining slowly erodes under the gentle current of negotiating on the merits. Coming into a conflictual situation as an uncritical advocate will guarantee ineffectual marginalization and a dismissive wave from at least one conflictual party. That may be emotionally satisfying for some, but the real work of avoiding misery calls for a more thorough, challenging strategy.

diversity is stability: the holy grail of coalition

"How can you buy or sell the sky, the warmth of the land? The idea is strange to us.

If we do not own the freshness of the air and the sparkle of the water, how can you buy them?

Every part of this earth is sacred to my people. Every shining pine needle, every sandy shore, every mist in the dark woods, every clearing and humming insect is holy in the memory and experience of my people. The sap which courses through the trees carries the memories of the red man...

All things are connected.

This we know. The earth does not belong to man; man belongs to the earth...

Our God is the same God. This earth is precious to him. Even the white man cannot be exempt from the common destiny.

—Chief Seattle, 1854 (Michalowski: 6-7)

A basic principle in the science of ecology is that diversity brings strength and stability. Scientists learned that first in the fields of plant geography, especially when integrated with various specialties in natural history. (Smith: 3) We see that principle in human society as well, with a mixture of cultures, colors, religions and abilities interacting to give any human venture a greater chance of long-term survival.

Another ecological principle is punctuated equilibrium, first posited and essentially proved by Eldredge and Gould back in 1972, and by Stanley in 1979. The nut of the concept is that evolution does not proceed on a gradual basis so much as occur by chance juxtaposition of mutation and duress. (Smith: 63-64) Thus, while the frog has little reason to evolve when it matches the niche it fills so perfectly, the environment can change, even cataclysmically, and those individuals who, for example, can survive a long drought because they are mutants who happened to be alive when one struck, live to reproduce, effectively replacing the formerly dominant frog "model" with a new, more adapted model.

Frogs are, indeed, a species which can teach humanity a great deal. Like coral (*Coelenterata*), they are dying off and suffering maladaptive mutations globally. They are, in some senses, a proof that we cannot palm off the ecological problems onto anyone, anywhere. There are no more demographically weak and politically strong areas, once we understand the lessons of transboundary pollution. To act in resonance with ecological principles, then, we ought to heed the advice of a woman who started as "just" a housewife and mother, then a local environmental activist, then a national and eventually international environmental protection leader. Rejecting the NIMBY (not in my backyard) model of local-only protectionism that tends to foist the problem onto others, Lois Gibbs proclaims the time for NOPE, "not on planet Earth." (Miller: 286) A local struggle is valuable, but much more so when linked to a wider effort to ban the problem altogether, not merely legislate or litigate it to relocate a toxic problem. A bombing range is no more appropriate in Scotland than in Puerto Rico (Environmental injustice in reverse, resulting from Puerto Rican protest over a US military proving range on the island of Vieques, now shifting its activities to Scotland under order of the Clinton administration.).

Within, or related to, these theories, is that of island biogeography, or insular ecology, posited by R. MacArthur and E. Wilson in 1967. It notes what Darwin found in the Galapagos—that speciation occurs to take advantage of unique ecosystems—and that the availability, size and richness of an ecosystem will determine its biodiversity. Thus, a small and less fertile island will exhibit a paucity of species; a big area easily reached with abundant natural resources will eventually come to a more diverse homeostasis, or stability of species. (Smith: 454-456)

Given these principles of ecology and others, we can infer that our human make-up ought not be monocultural, singular approach or dogmatically rigid in our attitude, but rather open to "experiments in truth," to borrow from Gandhi. In my opinion, we only make a mistake when we either employ violence or fail to learn from our actions. This, of course, implies reflection and communication, as well as willingness to claim error and the egolessness to try methods formerly discarded or disregarded. These ecological principles ought to help in multicultural appreciation and thus cross-cultural communication and coalition building. In short, we who wish to protect the Earth ought to be drawn to the same system that evolution has used every time it hazards another adaptation that may or may not succeed. It's also the scientific theory: hypothesis, experiment, new hypothesis, experiment, and so forth. Action, reflection, action.

Thus, while I hold that nonviolence is crucial and ought to be as absolute as can be attained, *nothing* else really is a *sine qua non* in our efforts to achieve peace between humans and the Earth. Contrary to common, popular, and even intuitive understanding, the rubric of nonviolence covers a huge panoply of possibilities. Once we begin closing off those myriad options—usually in the name of political correctness or religious rectitude—we almost certainly doom ourselves to failure. After all, we are not trying to preserve a dominant human paradigm as much as we are trying to preserve the Earth. One of those must take priority and one must be secondary, and it will not be the way the Earth runs its affairs. "Nature bats last," said Mo Udall, and, indeed, it is incumbent upon humans, as Santee Sioux poet John Trudell said, to understand our place and role in Creation and live that role properly. I assert that one of humankind's roles is to learn to live nonviolently and keep to its place in Creation or face extinction.

a New Republic of insects, grasses, humans

For humans to begin to develop an evolved method of conflict management, we ought to synthesize an eclectic array of elements from: indigenous economical lifeways; hard science understanding of ecological risk factors; new and more comprehensive definitions of security; and the nuggets of theory and practice of both conflict management and nonviolence. This will require changing the dogma of all four of those disciplines and will, possibly, result in a new approach that considers them all properly, in the new lights of each other.

The least effective way to practice nonviolence is in conjunction with a violent wing of the struggle; we have seen this in numerous liberation battles from the Philippines to El Salvador to Namibia to Guatemala to Columbia. In the US, we have seen what happened to Native peoples when they used violence. It became genocide against some tribes and, for a period between 1870-1890 in the American West, against virtually all tribes. The approach of the Quakers to the Delaware people and the Delaware response to them is instructive; William Penn negotiated a treaty with the tribes that brought peace and harmony for generations and avoided casualties on all sides. (Lynd: *xi-xv*, 1) Three centuries later, Native peoples reversed the direction of the lesson; the use of nonviolence in several Wisconsin and Michigan Anishinabe campaigns to win back their treaty rights and protect the Earth ought to give us a good North American model of Native-initiated nonviolence.

The most effective way to practice nonviolence is in conjunction with more complex negotiations, from courtroom to Congress, from education to statecraft, from backchannel proxy talk to transnational diplomacy. "Litigation and legislation in the service of the underclass cannot succeed without supportive mass action," says Arthur Kinoy, longtime attorney to movements dating from the 1950s, when he served Martin Luther King, Jr. (Kinoy) In the international arena, scholars generally note that non-governmental negotiations often succeed where nation-states have largely failed. (Starkey: 61) This ought to open a line of sight for those who wish to make a difference internationally with nonviolent action. Then that action ought to be considered a component of a much larger, more complex, campaign.

The elements of indigenous peoples' economical outlook that ought to be of significant value in our calculations of how to approach saving the Earth all involve the regard for each microecological system as a microeconomic management unit. Thus, each lake with wild rice becomes valuable not just for the general clean water but for an economical value far beyond dollars attached to rice sales. Protecting these lifeways is protecting the sustainable, sustenance economy that in turn is protecting rather than attacking the Earth. If making and preparing to make shooting wars is deeply injurious to these economies, these lifeways, then new methods of conflict management are called for. Nonviolence is in harmony with these lifeways; violence is not in the era of modern weaponry and hazardous production methods of those arsenals.

This analysis goes beyond the standard environmental or wilderness protection arguments and on to an appreciation of true ecological wisdom, that which includes humans as a part of the ecology, not as an intruding outsider. Some call this Indigenous Wisdom, some call it Deep Ecology, but the general thrust of those two bodies of knowledge and those two value systems generally ignores newer methods of conflict management even as the new diplomats seldom learn from indigenous economies, which is a fatal flaw in both schools of thought in our time.

Many of the human connections between basic human rights and the elimination of armed conflict were seen and noted by Martin Luther King, Jr. Had he lived—given his reach of mind, depth of universal compassion and willingness to grow—he would likely have made the environmental connections; his final, most mature year of life was devoted in no small measure to facilitating the links few were making privately and fewer were making publicly. His ability to synthesis and propose the new result was what made him a great thinker—and it's likely what got him executed.

The Riverside Church in New York is a place of great beauty, ornate and elegant structure, cathedral-like acoustics and labyrinthine substructures. It was there, on 4 April 1967, that the Reverend Martin Luther King, Jr. delivered his germinal "*Declaration of Independence from the War in Vietnam*." At the invitation of Clergy and Laity Concerned About the War in Vietnam, he spoke eloquently of the agony of speaking out as a member of a society that was just beginning to grant his people their human rights, the joy in finally being a part of a great and general religious opposition to a US war, and the growing realization that, in direct contradiction to the advice from friends and warnings from opponents, peace and civil rights *do* mix.

"*I come to this platform to make a passionate plea to my beloved nation*," said King. "*to my fellow Americans who, with me, bear the greatest responsibility in ending a conflict that has exacted a heavy price on both continents.*"

Today, I might guess, King would make the same assertion about the environment, about what the military has done to it, about what Native peoples have endured as a result, and about the relative preference for and efficacy of nonviolence as the alternative to armed conflict.

"*Perhaps*," King ventured, "*a new spirit is rising among us.*" (King: 36) Perhaps that is true again.

sources

Deming, Barbara, ***We Are All Part of One Another: A Barbara Deming Reader***. Philadelphia PA: New Society Publishers, 1984.

Fisher, Roger and William Ury, ***Getting to Yes: Negotiating Agreement Without Giving In***. NYC: Penguin Books 1981, 2nd edition, 1991.

King, Jr., Dr. Martin Luther, "Letter from Birmingham City Jail," open letter, 16 April 1963. Reprinted in ***Why We Can't Wait***. NYC: Harper & Row, 1963.

King, Jr., Dr. Martin Luther, "*Declaration of Independence from the War in Vietnam*," in Martin Luther King, Jr. Essay Series #1, NYC: A. J. Muste Memorial Institute.

Kinoy, Arthur, lecture, Northland College, 22 January 2000.

Koggel, Christine, ***Moral Issues in Global Perspective***. Peterborough, Ontario CAN: Broadview Press, 1999.

Kriesberg, Louis, ***Constructive Conflict: From Escalation to Resolution***. Lanham MD: Rowman & Littlefield, 1998.

Lynd, Staughton and Alice Lynd, ***Nonviolence in America: A Documentary History***. Maryknoll NY: Orbis Books, 1995.

Miall, Hugh, et al., ***Contemporary Conflict Resolution***. Cambridge UK: Polity Press, 1999.

Michalowski, Helen, ***The Power of the People: Active Nonviolence in the United States***. Philadelphia: New Society Publishers, 1987.

Miller, Jr., G. Tyler, ***Environmental Science: Sustaining the Earth, third edition***. Belmont CA: Wadsworth Publishing Company, 1991.

Shrader-Frechette, Kristin, "Practical Ecology and Foundations for Environmental

Ethics," in Koggel, Christine, ***Moral Issues in Global Perspective.*** Peterborough, Ontario CAN: Broadview Press, 1999.

Smith, Robert Leo, ***Elements of Ecology second edition***. NYC: Harper & Row, 1986.

Starkey, Brigid, et alia, ***Negotiating a Complex World: An Introduction to International Negotiation***. Boston: Rowman & Littlefield, 1999.

appendix 1: environmental law in coastal waters~~~

At times, laws exist and are ignored by corporations, the military, the media and the courts. This is just one small body of law that the citizenry and its media ought to know, given here as an example of what might be available. The United States Coast Guard has environmental enforcement obligations, among them:

- The Refuse Act, 1894, prohibits dumping of refuse in shoreline waters or on shores of US navigable waters.
- The Federal Water Pollution Control Act, 1972, AKA Clean Water Act, prohibits dumping of oils and hazardous substances.
- Oil Pollution Act, 1990, prohibits oil spills, creates fund for clean-up.
- Comprehensive Environmental Response Compensation And Liability Act, AKA Superfund.
- MARPOL 73/78, international law, criminalizing oil spills and hazardous substance dumping.

source

United States Coast Guard, "Coast Guard enforces federal pollution laws to protect Lake Superior," *Budgeteer News*, 7 March 1999: B5.

appendix 2: leading recipients of US military training, 1998~~~

The worldwide market for US arms is pursued aggressively and with the massive assistance of Congress and the Pentagon. The potential customers are often dictatorial within the borders of their own nation, suppressing unions, eliminating environmental law enforcement and killing indigenous leadership when minority rights are demanded. A part of the salesmanship practiced by these arms merchants is a guarantee of free training, courtesy of the US taxpayer. Thus, Lockheed Martin can sell a warplane at a handsome profit, fattened by an avoidance of training costs for the customer, since you and I pay for that training straight out of our income tax. Next time you feel that phantom pain from a missing part, look at your paycheck statement. You'll have a new appreciation for the term "stub."

- ☹ Columbia, currently killing its indigenous people, got $900,000 in military training from our Pentagon.
- ☹ Indonesia, whose armed forces proved capable of 25 years of genocide against the indigenous of East Timor, received $800,000 of free military training from the US in 1998.
- ☹ Mexico, which has militarized Chiapas and slaughtered villagers at Acteal, got a cool million in US military training last year.
- ☹ Turkey, famous for killing of Kurds, was the lucky recipient of $1.5 million in such training in 1998. The list goes on. (Lumpe: 19)

source:

Lumpe, Lora & Jeff Donarski, ***The Arms Trade Revealed: A Guide for Investigators and Activists***. Washington DC: Federation of American Scientists, 1998.

bibliography~~~

Andregg, Michael, ***On the Causes of War***. Minneapolis MN: Ground Zero Minnesota, 1996.

Barash, David, ***Approaches to Peace: A Reader in Peace Studies***. New York: Oxford University Press, 2000.

Begich, Dr. Nick and Jeane Manning, ***Angels Don't Play This HAARP: Advances in Tesla Technology***. Anchorage AK: 1995.

Brown, Michael E. and Richard N. Rosecrance, editors, ***The Costs of Conflict: Prevention and Cure in the Global Arena***. Lanham MD: Rowman & Littlefield Publishers, Inc., 1999.

Burroughs, John, ***The (Il)legality of Threat or Use of Nuclear Weapons: A Guide to the Historic Opinion of the International Court of Justice***. Munster, Germany: LIT, 1997.

Catalinotto, John, and Sara Flounders, editors, ***Metal of Dishonor, Depleted Uranium: How the Pentagon Radiates Soldiers and Civilians with DU Weapons***. NYC: International Action Center, 1999 (original 1997).

Center for Defense Information, ***1997 CDI Military Almanac***. Washington DC: CDI, 1997.

——, ***1999 CDI Military Almanac***. Washington DC: CDI, 1999.

Collette, Will, ***Dealing With Military Toxics***. Falls Church VA: Citizen's Clearinghouse for Hazardous Wastes Inc., 1987.

Congressional Quarterly, ***The Middle East, Ninth Edition***. Washington DC: CQ Press, 2000.

Cortright, David and George A. Lopez, ***The Sanctions Decade: Assessing UN Strategies in the 1990s***. Boulder CO: Lynne Rienner Publishers, 2000.

Coyle, Dana, et al., ***Deadly Defense: Military Radioactive Landfills***. NYC: Radioactive Waste Campaign, 1988.

Deming, Barbara, ***We Are All Part of One Another: A Barbara Deming Reader***. Philadelphia PA: New Society Publishers, 1984.

Dewes, Kate and Robert Green, ***Aotearoa/New Zealand at the World Court***. Christchurch, New Zealand: Raven Press, 1999.

Dycus, Stephen, ***National Defense and the Environment***. Hanover NH: University Press of New England, 1996.

Ehrlich, Anne H and John W. Birks, editors, ***Hidden Dangers: Environmental Consequences of Preparing for War***. San Francisco: Sierra Club Books, 1990.

Eichstaedt, Peter H., ***If You Poison Us: Uranium and Native Americans***. Santa Fe NM: Red Crane Books, 1994.

Elhance, Arun P., ***Hydropolitics in the 3rd World: Conflict and Cooperation in***

International River Basins. Washington DC: United States Institute of Peace, 1999.

Fahey, Dan, ***Depleted Uranium Exposures: Case Narrative***, 3rd edition. San Francisco: Swords to Plowshares, 1998.

Falla, Ricardo, ***Massacres in the Jungle: Ixcán, Guatemala, 1975-1982***. Boulder CO: Westview Press, 1994.

Fellman, Gordon, ***Rambo and the Dalai Lama: The Compulsion to Win and Its Threat to Human Survival***. Albany NY: State University of New York Press, 1998.

Fisher, Roger and William Ury, ***Getting to Yes: Negotiating Agreement Without Giving In***. NYC: Penguin Books 1981, 2nd edition, 1991.

Fisk, Larry & John Schellenberg, editors, ***Patterns of Conflict: Paths to Peace***, Peterborough, Ontario: Broadview Press, 2000.

Foerstel, Lenora, ***Creating Surplus Populations: The Effect of Military and Corporate Policies on Indigenous Peoples***. Washington DC: Maisonneuve Press, 1996.

Gerber, Michele Stenehjem, ***On the Home Front: The Cold War Legacy of the Hanford Nuclear Site***. Lincoln NE: University of Nebraska Press, 1992.

Gleick, Peter H., ***The World's Water: The Biennial Report of Freshwater Resources 1998 1999***. Washington DC: Island Press, 1998.

Hanh, Thich Nhat, ***Love in Action: Writings on Nonviolent Social Change***. Berkeley CA: Parallax Press, 1993.

Harding, Vincent, ***Martin Luther King: The Inconvenient Hero***. Maryknoll NY: Orbis Books, 1996.

Harney, Corbin, ***The Way It Is: One Water...One Air...One Mother Earth...***. Nevada City CA: Blue Dolphin Publishing, 1995.

Holbrooke, Richard, ***To End a War***. NYC: Random House, Modern Library, 1999.

Homer-Dixon, Thomas F. and Jessica Blitt, editors, ***Ecoviolence: Links Among Environment, Population, and Security***. Lanham MD: Rowman & Littlefield Publishers, 1998.

Homer-Dixon, Thomas F., ***Environment, Scarcity, and Violence***. Princeton NJ: Princeton University Press, 1999.

Kennedy, Paul, ***The Rise and Fall of the Great Powers: Economic Change and Military Conflict from 1500 to 2000***. NYC: Random House, 1987.

King, Jr., Dr. Martin Luther, ***Why We Can't Wait***. NYC: Harper & Row, 1963.

Koggel, Christine, ***Moral Issues in Global Perspective.*** Peterborough, Ontario CAN: Broadview Press, 1999.

Kyi, Aung San Suu, ***The Voice of Hope: Conversations with Alan Clements***. NYC: Seven Stories Press, 1997.

Lac Courte Oreilles Tribe, ***Mitigation Plan of the Lac Courte Oreilles Indian Tribe of Wisconsin Concerning the U.S. Navy's Project ELF***. Hayward WI: Lac Courte Oreilles Tribe, 2000.

LaDuke, Winona, ***All Our Relations: Native Struggles for Land and Life***. Cambridge MA: South End Press, 1999.

Libby, Ronald T., ***Eco-Wars: Political Campaigns and Social Movements***. NYC: Columbia University Press, 1998.

Lumpe, Lora & Jeff Donarski, ***The Arms Trade Revealed: A Guide for Investigators and Activists***. Washington DC: Federation of American Scientists, 1998.

Lynd, Staughton and Alice Lynd, ***Nonviolence in America: A Documentary History***. Maryknoll NY: Orbis Books, 1995.

Morgan, Larry Cloud, ***Prison Meditations***, Minneapolis: St. Joseph's House, 1985.

Miall, Hugh, et al., ***Contemporary Conflict Resolution: The Prevention, Management and Transformation of Deadly Conflicts***. Cambridge UK: Polity Press, 1999.

Michalowski, Helen, ***The Power of the People: Active Nonviolence in the United States***. Philadelphia: New Society Publishers, 1987.

Miller, Jr., G. Tyler, ***Environmental Science: Sustaining the Earth, third edition***. Belmont CA: Wadsworth Publishing Company, 1991.

Nesaule, Agate, ***A Woman in Amber: Healing and Trauma of War and Exile***. NYC: Penguin Books, 1995.

O'Reilly, Ciaron, ***Bomber Grounded, Runway Closed: Prison Letters and Court Notes of a Gulf War Resister***. Marion SD: Rose Hill Books, 1994.

Ornstein, Robert, and Paul Ehrlich, ***New World New Mind: Moving Toward Conscious Evolution*** NYC: Doubleday, 1989.

Peterson, Jeannie, editor, ***The Aftermath: The Human and Ecological Consequences of Nuclear War***. NYC: Pantheon Books, 1983.

Plant, Judith, editor, ***Healing the Wounds: The Promise of Ecofeminism***. Philadelphia PA: New Society Publishers, 1989.

Rabinovich, Itamar, ***Waging Peace: Israel and the Arabs and the End of the Century***. NYC: Farrar, Strauss and Giroux, 1999.

Reardon, Betty, ***Women and Peace: Feminist Visions of Global Security***. Albany NY: State University of New York Press, 1993.

Rekmans, Lorraine, Keith Lewis and Anabel Dwyer, ***This Is My Homeland: Stories of the Effects of Nuclear Industries by People of the Serpent River First Nation and the North Shore of Lake Huron.*** Cutler, Ontario, Canada: Serpent River First Nation, 1999.

Ringler, Dick, et al., editors, ***Dilemmas of War and Peace: A Sourcebook***. Madison WI: University of Wisconsin, 1993.

Romero, Oscar, ***The Violence of Love***. Farmington PA: The Plough Publishing House, 1998 (original 1988, Harper & Row Publishers)

Salem, Paul, editor, ***Conflict Resolution in the Arab World: Selected Essays***. Beirut, Lebanon: American University of Beirut, 1997.

Sharp, Gene, ***The Politics of Nonviolent Action***. Boston: Porter Sargent Publishers, 1973.

Shiva, Vandana, ***Close to Home: Women Reconnect Ecology, Health and Development Worldwide***. Philadelphia: New Society Publishers, 1994.

Sivard, Ruth Leger, ***World Military and Social Expenditures 1996***. Washington DC: World Priorities, 1996.

Smith, Robert Leo, ***Elements of Ecology second edition***. NYC: Harper & Row, 1986.

Soffer, Aaron, ***Rivers of Fire: The Conflicts Over Water in the Middle East***. Lanham MD: Rowman & Littlefield, 1999.

Starkey, Brigid, et alia, ***Negotiating a Complex World: An Introduction to International Negotiation***. Boston: Rowman & Littlefield, 1999.

Sutherland, Bill and Matt Meyer, ***Guns and Gandhi in Africa: Pan African Insights on Nonviolence, Armed Struggle and Liberation in Africa***. Trenton NJ: Africa World Press, Inc, 2000.

Taylor, Paul, ***See How They Run: Electing the President in an Age of Mediaocracy***. NYC: Alfred A. Knopf, 1990.

Terkel, Susan Neiburg, ***People Power: A Look at Nonviolent Action and Defense***. NYC: Lodestar, 1996.

Thomas, William, ***Bringing the War Home***. Anchorage AK: Earthpulse Press Incorporated, 1998.

——, ***Scorched Earth: The Military's Assault on the Environment***. Gabriola Island, Vancouver, British Columbia: New Society Press, 1995.

Tromp, H.W. & G.R. LaRocque, editors, ***Nuclear War in Europe***. Groningen, Denmark: Groningen University Press, 1981

United Nations Development Programme, ***Human Development Report 1996***. New York: Oxford University Press, Inc., 1996.

United Nations Environment Programme, ***The Kosovo Conflict: Consequences for the Environment & Human Settlements***. Nairobi, Kenya: UNEP, 1999.

Westing, Arthur H., editor, ***Herbicides in War: The Long-term Ecological and Human Consequences***. London: Taylor & Francis, 1984

——, ***Environmental Warfare: A Technical, Legal and Policy Appraisal***. London: Taylor & Francis, 1984

——, ***Explosive Remnants of War: Mitigating the Environmental Effects***. London: Taylor & Francis, 1985.

——., editor, ***Global Resources and International Conflict: Environmental Factors in Strategic Policy and Action***. NYC: Oxford University Press, 1986.

——., editor, ***Cultural Norms, War and the Environment***. NYC: Oxford University Press, 1988.

Wheelwright, Philip, editor, ***The Presocratics***. NYC: Macmillan Publishing Company, 1966.

White, Jonathan R., ***Terrorism: An Introduction***. 2nd edition. New York: West/ Wadsworth Publishing, 1998.

Worldwatch Institute, ***State of the World 1992***. New York: W.W. Norton & Company Ltd., 1992.

——, ***State of the World 1995***. New York: W.W. Norton & Company Ltd., 1995.

——, ***State of the World 1996***. New York: W.W. Norton & Company Ltd., 1996.

——, ***State of the World 1997***. New York: W.W. Norton & Company Ltd., 1997.

——, ***State of the World 2000***. New York: W.W. Norton & Company Ltd., 2000.

World Resources Institute, ***World Resources: 1998-1999***. New York: World Resources Institute, 1998.

index~~~

Tom H. Hastings is Coördinator of the Peace, Conflict and Global Studies program at Northland, an environmental liberal arts college on the shores of Lake Superior in northern Wisconsin, US. He can be reached at:

Northland College, 1411 Ellis Av., Ashland WI 54806
715.682-1250
thastings@northland.edu

p 54 100 hr. attack

windbreak - man later
spectated - support guards